SENTENCING
IN
TIME

Linda Ross Meyer

Public Works — AUSTIN D. SARAT *Series Editor*

Conceived as a "digital pamphlet" series, titles in *Public Works* seek out and make available to a wide audience of readers the perspectives of leading scholars in the humanities on questions rising to significance in our public conversation, and demanding more discerning examination and penetrating insight. Shorter than monographs, these works offer both authors and readers the freedom of long-form essays and the tools of digital media to see through the lens of the human experience the seemingly intractable questions confronting a complex, deeply interconnected, and sometimes shockingly violent world.

Essays published in *Public Works* series are available as open-access works of scholarship, immediately and freely available to readers and thinkers everywhere. As digital works, they will be published to the web and also downloadable to a variety of reading devices.

SENTENCING IN TIME

Published by The Amherst College Press
Robert Frost Library • Amherst, Massachusetts

ISBN 978-1-943208-08-1 paperback
ISBN 978-1-943208-09-8 electronic book

Library of Congress Control Number: 2017953612

The manuscript of this work was peer reviewed in a double-blind process prior to publication.

Table of Contents

Acknowledgments

I wish to thank my wonderful colleagues and editors at Amherst College, Quinnipiac University School of Law, the Association for the Study of Law, Culture, and the Humanities, and my hosts at Pace Law School and the University of Miami, for their time and thoughtful comments. Omissions and errors left uncorrected or forgotten remain the responsibility of myself at time t+1.

We live in deeds, not years.

—*Philip James Bailey*

Introduction

In the Museum of Natural History in New York, there is a slice of a tree. The tree rings begin more than a thousand years before the establishment of the United States. Museum goers can see all the rings at once and count them, finding the years of drought and fire, determining which came before and which after. But these are marks of time, as though time could be seen all at once and expressed as a picture or a number, and neither we, nor the tree, can experience this time "as passing."

Several months ago, I was sitting in a coffee shop, when in walked a friend of mine from high school. I smiled and tried to catch his eye, but when he gave me a puzzled look, I realized, blushing, that he could not be my friend from high school. The person who had walked into the coffee shop was only 19 or 20 years old. My high school friend would be 53. But I had forgotten that he had continued to age while I was not looking.

I once spoke with a woman whose brother had been brutally murdered a decade earlier. She was speaking all over the country on behalf of an organization to abolish the death penalty. I asked her whether she would ever consider meeting with the man who murdered her brother. She could have the chance to tell him of her family's suffering, to find out what he had done in prison, and perhaps to hear him express remorse or apology. She thought hard for a minute, her face taut with pain, clearly fighting with herself, wanting to be able to say "yes." "No," she said, finally. She explained that the crime was something she had tried hard to put out of her life, "like a box on the top shelf, far in the back of a closet." She wanted it to be out of her world, no longer part of her day-to-day reality. "I don't ever want to open that box again," she said.

Occasionally, I teach at a prison. The reason I was originally moved to do so was that, during a prison visit with one of my classes, I met a young woman serving a 50-year sentence for a crime she committed at age 14. "I've tried to commit suicide several times," she told me. "It's such a huge amount of time. I just feel sometimes that I don't have a reason to get out of bed in the morning." Another woman with a life sentence chimed in, "That's right. After a while, you don't do the time; the time does you."

🕒

Paul Ricoeur writes of the *aporia* between two philosophical accounts of time: "cosmological time" and "phenomenological time," that is, between time understood as a measurement of duration based on some form of steady movement (whether that "tick" is based on the day/night cycle, the movement of sand through a small aperture, the half-life of carbon-14, or the movement of electrons around a nucleus), and time understood as the experienced relationship among expectation, perception, and memory.[1]

One aspect of phenomenological time is that it does not seem to pass, and people do not change, except as we perceive them to pass before us. As in the examples above, when we are not present to perceive the change, people and events remain "frozen" in time in our memories. We often take up with old friends "as if no time has passed," because we often fail to acknowledge that any time *has* passed or that any change has occurred. And we "put things behind us" and move on, forgetting that the people "behind us" continue to change while we are not looking. Past and future are always in relation to the "now" of a human understanding, and the experienced now is always inflected by the "expected" based on the remembered, as in the example of seeing the old friend in the cafe.

---

1. In describing perception, Ricoeur draws on the notions of "protention" and "retention" in German philosopher Edmund Husserl's phenomenology. See Paul Ricoeur, *Time and Narrative*, vol. III, Kathleen Blamey and David Pellauer, trans. (Chicago: University of Chicago Press, 1988), 31-42.

A second aspect of phenomenological time is that it is not regular. Time slows down and speeds up. The young experience time as having a longer duration than the older do. High school lasts forever; graduate school seems much shorter. Traumatic experience may stop time, erase time, or create repetitive time. Exciting events pass more quickly than boring ones; happy times pass more quickly than sad ones. Time may be turgid with loss, or pregnant with anticipation. And "time in" is experienced differently in prison than on the outside. Some of those serving long sentences experience time as endlessly rewinding, as treadmill repetition and routine create identical days, months, and years. And even among those inside, time is experienced differently when one is closer to release than when the light at the end of the tunnel is merely a pinprick.[2]

By contrast, when we think of time "cosmologically," time is not tied to our *perception* of change, but exists as "having to do with" a regular, repeated motion, "even though we must continually extend our search for the absolute clock."[3] By positing some kind of cosmic moving metronome as our standard of measurement of time, we imagine time as an x-axis extending into infinity like number itself, entirely separate from human experience. Time becomes a linear substrate that can be cut into equal, quantifiable segments by the duration of some standard motion: "Change (movement) is in every case in the thing that changes (moves), whereas time is everywhere in everything equally."[4] From the cosmological perspective, we imagine time from the point of view of eternity, publicly present for us "all at once" and everywhere as a quantity, or time-line, or map of succession—or a display of tree rings.

Time understood cosmologically is, therefore, expressed as a contemporaneously-experienced visual or spatial numerical "truth." From the cosmological point of view, we can talk of successions of events, the "number of motion in respect to before and after," and, therefore,

2. See Stanton Wheeler, "Socialization in Correctional Institutions," *American Sociological Review* 26 (1961): 697–712. I am grateful to an anonymous reviewer for this citation. More recent scholarship shows a similar non-linear relation between sentence length and infractions in prison. See Elisa L. Toman, et al., "The Implications of Sentence Length for Inmate Adjustment to Prison Life," *Journal of Criminal Justice* 43 (2015): 510–521.

3. Ricoeur, *Time and Narrative* vol. III, 13.

4. Ibid., 14, explicating Aristotle's *Physics*.

cause and effect; but we lose the explicitly durational ideas of "then" (before now), "now," and "later" (after now).[5] The "now" requires a being *in* time that is not available from the cosmological perspective *outside* time, looking at time.[6]

When we think of time cosmologically we regard time from the perspective of a god, who sees temporal relationships "all at once" rather than as "passing from one to another." Cosmological time is like sorting old pictures into chronological order on a screen, and seeing them all in a row "at once" in the proper order of succession. Or, to use a different metaphor, it is like the sheet music that all-at-once represents the succession of notes in their measured order. Phenomenological time, by contrast, is a lived present of a slide-show experience that passes from one picture to another—now, and then now, and then now. Or, it is the playing or hearing of music in performance.[7] Visual metaphors, like the time-line, predominate when we speak of cosmological time; auditory metaphors, like St. Augustine's example of chanting a psalm, predominate when we speak of phenomenological time.[8]

According to Ricoeur, each of these two accounts of time corrects a problem with the other, and each creates its own unique philosophical difficulty. Cosmological accounts of time correct the misperception that time is identical with perception (and the misperception that what is unperceived does not change). Yet this cosmological account of time seems to fail to capture the passing before us and the experience of duration that we associate with time. Phenomenological understandings of time, on the other hand, call attention to the first-person experience of the passing of time, its interpenetrated and durational character as past, present, and future, and correct the misconception that humans in time can understand time from a point of view of eternity. But phenomenological time cannot encompass, for example, an idea

5. Aristotle, *Physics*, Book IV, 219b.

6. Ricoeur, *Time and Narrative* vol. III, 19.

7. Cf. ibid., 19–21.

8. St. Augustine, *Confessions*, trans. Henry Chadwick (New York: Oxford University Press, 1991), Book XI, xxvii (36), 242.

of geological time that extends apart from or before the origins of human life.[9]

The thesis of this essay is that the way in which we think and talk in the criminal law context about sentencing people to "time" exhibits both temporal fallacies. We fall into the phenomenological mistake of forgetting that time continues to pass in prison (while "we" are not looking), and when we think or talk of those serving time (if we think of them at all), we "freeze-frame" the prisoner as though, like Sleeping Beauty, no time has passed since the crime occurred.

Not only do we make phenomenological mistakes in sentencing, but in calculating sentences, we make the cosmological mistake of treating "time" abstractly as a mere "number," and we treat sentences as "debts" that can mount far beyond the finite time of a human life, as though the debt could be paid "all at once" like a mortgage: 50 years, 50 cents, 50 dollars, 50 cookies. We don't think of 50 as having a duration, just a quantity. In part this mistake is due to the persistence of retribution as our default theory of punishment; we believe that time must be measured by and match the crime. In consequence, the crime is always recalled fresh-frozen to our minds as the measure of sentencing, i.e., time as a quantity commensurate with the crime.

In making both phenomenological and cosmological errors, we also forget that we should understand that time is the realm or mode in which humans act and understand as we finite creatures grow, change, learn to connect and explain the disarray of past events, and then project that story into a future. Hence, if punishment is to have a "meaning" (such as, retribution or atonement), then the "time" a punishment takes is only a frame within which meaningful human action happens. It is the human action in time that may have meaning, not the time itself. Instead, then, of sentencing people to "time," if we continue to require that the imposition of state punishment have a justification or "rational basis" (as our constitutional law requires), we should sentence people to acts, rather than to "time," assuming that we need to sentence them at all.[10]

---

9. Ricoeur, *Time and Narrative* vol. III, 19–21.

10. George Pavlich has argued persuasively that "accusation" itself and the characterization of actions as "wrongs" needs a great deal more philosophical attention,

I. The phenomenological fallacy: Out of sight, out of time

We tend to imagine prisoners as living a kind of time-warp existence "in a box on the back top shelf of the closet." And that thought is comforting and safe—a guarantee to trauma victims that the trauma will not recur. But to the one living in that box, how is that time experienced? What meaning does it have? Is that time "punishment"?

The phenomenological account of time, originating with St. Augustine, equates time with perception, memory and expectation:

> It is in you, O my mind, that I measure time. Do not bring against me, do not bring against yourself the disorderly throng of your impressions. In you, I say, I measure time. What I measure is the impress produced in you by things as they pass and abiding in you when they have passed: and it is present. I do not measure the things themselves whose passage produced the impress; it is the impress that I measure when I measure time. Thus either that is what time is, or I am not measuring time at all."[11]

But that which exists in memory, as Augustine's "impress," seems to become either "eternalized" or forgotten, and, ironically, the sense of time as *passing* is lost, except in the perceiver's "now." When we lock those convicted of crimes out of sight, we lock them out of mind, and consequently, out of (perceived) time.

When we think "retributively," the "impress" of the crime is eternalized in memory, and the repetition of the trauma is brought fresh to mind, as any sentence must always be measured by the *actus reus* (the objective element of a crime) and *mens rea* (the subjective state of mind of the person who commits the crime) as they were *at that moment* and only that moment, regardless of what came before or after. Hence, retribution requires a time-consciousness that "freeze-frames" and isolates the memory of the crime, like the sometimes-haunting moment of trauma that it might have been.

---

and certainly the problem of "overcriminalization" has been a concern for a long time. George Pavlich, "Apparatuses of Criminal Accusation" in George Pavlich and Matthew P. Unger, eds., Accusation: Creating Criminals (Vancouver: University of British Columbia Press, 2016). See Sanford Kadish, "The Crisis of Overcriminalization," Annals of the American Academy of Political and Social Science 374 (1967), 157.

11   St. Augustine, *Confessions*, Book XI, xxvii (36), 242.

For example, in *United States v. Pepper*, an appellate court reversed a sentencing court's leniency and sent the case back for resentencing. By the time of the resentencing hearing, the defendant had already completed his original prison term, and was employed, sober, and going to college. The sentencing court took those factors into account on resentencing, and refused to give the defendant more prison time. The government appealed the sentence a second time, and the appellate court again remanded on the ground that the sentencing judge should not have taken into account, on resentencing, any information that was not available at the time of the original sentencing. The result of this opinion (had the Supreme Court not intervened) would have been that the defendant, despite having turned his life around, would have been sent back to prison, because none of his excellent post-sentencing conduct was relevant to resentencing. According to the Eighth Circuit Court of Appeals, the "fit" between crime and sentence was to be determined at the time of sentencing, and the "appropriate sentence" was frozen at that time.[12]

Yet when we think about "doing time" from the perspective of the imprisoned person, we are not content to "freeze-frame" time in this way. J. C. Oleson suggested many years ago, tongue-in-cheek, that we give those convicted of crimes the choice of a medically-induced "punitive coma" for the period of their sentence, then return the reawakened prisoner, at the end of the sentence, Rip Van Winkle-style, to the waking world.[13] Oleson argued, with chilling conviction, that we would thereby extract the "time due" from an offender at less expense and without any of the prison rape, abuse, over-crowding, cruelty, and conscious suffering now endemic to imprisonment. If what matters is that a certain quantity of time be deducted from a person's life as their punishment, then Oleson's proposal would seem apt.

But, of course, the punitive coma seems simultaneously like too much punishment and no punishment at all. And that is Oleson's point. The thought experiment leads us to question why and in what way "time" constitutes a punishment. Our sense that someone in a coma

---

12. United States v. Pepper, 518 F.3d 939 (8th Cir. 2008); *Pepper v. United States*, 562 U.S. 476 (2011), 570 F. 3d 958, vacated in part, affirmed in part, and remanded.

13. J. C. Oleson, "The Punitive Coma," *California Law Review* 90:3 (2002), 829.

is not "doing time" because they do not perceive the passage of time reveals that "doing time" must be more than, or different from, merely persisting in time.

Ricoeur's account of time in association with narrative expands the limits of St. Augustine's phenomenological account, presenting the human experience of time as a kind of reflective narration that does not "freeze frame" memory and is at every moment a kind of story-telling, not a persisting or even a merely perceiving experience:

> The present is both what we are living and what realizes the expectations of a remembered past. In turn, this realization is inscribed in memory; I remember, having expected what is now realized. This realization is, henceforth, part of the meaning of the remembered expectation…. The possibility of turning to a memory and of sighting in it the expectations that were or were not realized later, contributes to inserting the memory within the unitary flow of lived experience.[14]

In other words, a meaningful human life experience requires a storyline of realized or unrealized expectations, a projection from past into future that presently refigures the past, a constant "there and back again," a plan or project or intention that is active, not passive, even when curtailed or forestalled or disappointed. Living "in time" is learning to expect, planning toward a future, and reinterpreting a past expectation in light of a present experience. There is no "freeze-framing," even of memory. For example, as soon as I realize that I have "mistaken" the young man in the cafe for an old friend, my memory of my old friend is "updated" accordingly.

And, of course, we reject Oleson's coma scenario in part because we believe that an offender's active reflection on and reassessment of the past in the present for the future is part of what "doing time" is supposed to involve as punishment. Without the active engagement "in time" with memory, doing time loses meaning.[15] Yet we forget the "ac-

---

14. Ricoeur, *Time and Narrative*, vol. III, 36.

15. Patricia Ewick recognizes the problem of "timelessness" especially in the context of incapacitation. She writes: "[Incapacitation] can never once and for all fulfill its own objectives. There is no conceivable point in time at which we would say, 'He is, finally, incapacitated enough.' The future about which we are so anxiously oriented, in which some hypothetical crime might occur, is not something we are moving toward nor is it something we are trying to change or avert. Rather, it is something we are running from, endlessly and in place." Patricia Ewick, "Time, Imagination, and Punishment," in *Punitive*

tivity" involved in living in time, because we fall into a second kind of cosmological fallacy that conceptualizes time as a thing with quantity.

🕐

II. The cosmological fallacy: Time is a thing with quantity

The cosmological understanding of time is our default mode—the time displayed on our watches and clocks. We normally imagine time to be the infinite substrate of existence subdivided by the ticking of a universal clock, the endless circling of the sun, the constant flowing of a perennial stream, or the endlessness of counting numbers. We imagine an infinity of time, like an endless number line stretching across an infinite space.

But the cosmological account of time will not do, either. We humans can't see time "all at once" as a number-line or as an amount of some "thing" that is infinite. A being that could know the world "outside of time" would not experience the world *as a flowing sequence of revelations and changes*, as we do, but would see it instead as an unchanging whole available all at once, in another kind of freeze-frame. The essence of time as *passing* seems lost to this cosmological account. I say, "It is May 12, 2015, at 8:55 in the morning." Saying this, I have thereby located the "now" in an infinite timeline, as a conceivable amount, frozen and present and stilled. I have "dropped a pin" on the map of time, as though a moment were a "thing" in a "place." But time is not a thing in a place that we can "see" all at once, "out" of time.

Despite the fact that we live in time, grammar often leads us to speak as though we were atemporal. Grammar allows us both to use "thing" and "place" as metaphors for time, and also imagines "thing" and "place" without reference to time. For example, English "freezes" nouns in timelessness. Unlike verbs, nouns and pronouns are not inflected with the passage of time—they are not inflected with tense. For example, "I ran, I run, I will run," but the "I" remains the same. I can speak of myself "in my girlhood, my womanhood, and my old

Imagination: Law, Justice, and Responsibility, ed. Austin Sarat (Tuscaloosa, Ala.: Alabama University Press, 2014): 162–63.

age," but I have to use a different noun for each stage, creating discontinuities instead of a sense of change or *passing*. Imagine if the continuum of growing and changing were reflected in grammar. Imagine if we thought of people, and nouns, as existing temporally and not as timeless substances.

There are a few languages that inflect nouns with tense, but not most familiar ones. [16] English, in a few cases, uses a clumsy type of temporal inflection, like, "ex-roommate," "ex-husband," and "ex-Kansan," to reflect an identity or relationship that was and is no longer. We also, of course, speak of "ex-offenders." We do not speak of "ex-victims," but rather, at least if the victim is still alive, of "survivors," a completely different term. In these common English usages, "ex" also seems to rely on spatial metaphors. Ex-wives and husbands are no longer *in* a marriage; ex-Kansans are no longer *in* Kansas, ex-cops are no longer *in* the force. For example, could we speak of an "ex-offender" who was not yet out of prison? "Ex-offender" usually means someone who is *out*. Again, the "ex" seems spatial—as in, "out of prison," rather than as denoting one who offended in the past but is not presently or is no longer committing crimes. Our terms "offender" and "ex-offender" seem to presume that one in prison is, indeed, *in* a box of unchanging substance with an indefinite shelf life ("offender") until he or she "gets out" ("ex-offender").

Jonathan Goldberg–Hiller has written of the temporal ambivalence that occurs when people serving time face a parole hearing. [17] On the one hand, they are charged with conjuring presently appearing remorse, often for a crime decades old. On the other hand, they must demonstrate that they are other than they were—a "new person," an "ex-offender." [18] How can the "new person" be remorseful for the "old

---

16. Tariana, an Amazonian language, is believed to have this characteristic. See Alexandra Y. Aikhenvald, *The Tariana language of Northwest Amazonia* (Cambridge: Cambridge University Press, 2003); and Rachel Nordlinger and Louisa Sadler, "The Syntax and Semantics of Tensed Nominals" in *Proceedings of the LFG03 Conference*, eds. Miriam Butt and Tracy Holloway King (Albany, NY: CSLI Publications, 2003) 328–346.

17. Jonathan Goldberg–Hiller, "Time and Punishment," *Quinnipiac Law Review* 31 (2013), 621-659.

18. In a letter submitted to the Connecticut Sentencing Commission, "Rachel," serving a fifty-year sentence without the chance of parole for an offense committed at age 14, wrote, "I don't believe that just because you are young your behaviors should be excused, but I

person's" crime? Moreover, the "new person" now sees the pre-existing circumstances and temptations that led to the "old person's" crime (drug abuse, trauma, lack of communication skills, etc.), and can demonstrate how they have "overcome" those obstacles. But at the same time, the "new person" must not mitigate their own responsibility for the crime or seem to be expressing an "excuse." The parole petitioner is put in the bind of arguing all at once what is, if considered as the atemporal act of a single unchanging "I," the illogical equivalent of: "I wasn't there, and if I were, I didn't do it, and if I did it, I am really sorry for it." But if grammar allowed us temporal inflection, the sentence would not be so illogical: "I (at time t+2) wasn't there, and though I (at time t) was, I (at time t-1) was not fully responsible, and when I (at time t) did it, I (at time t+1) am really sorry for it, and I (at time t+2) regret that it happened."

Grammar tricks us, as Nietzsche said.[19] Language enables us to "freeze frame" things in order to hold them in our minds and think and talk about them. Through language we can collate our impressions and memories of "the bed" yesterday, today, and tomorrow as the "same" bed, existing through time. "Time" itself is likewise a handy, steady, noun that enables us to think and talk about duration and "change" (also and ironically an unchanging noun). Casting experiences of the world as nouns, and thinking of nouns as things that endure in solidity and definition as timeless "things" is a kind of grammatical battle-cry against human temporality.[20]

---

can tell you that no 14-year-old child is the same person as a 30-year-old man or woman." Quoted in *Youth Matters: A Second Look for Connecticut's Children Serving Long Prison Sentences* (Hamden and New Haven, Conn.: Quinnipiac Civil Justice Clinic and Yale Allard K. Lowenstein International Human Rights Clinic, March 2013).

19. "'Reason' in language: Oh what a deceitful old woman! I am afraid we are not getting rid of God because we still believe in grammar." Friedrich Nietzsche, *Twilight of the Idols and The Anti-Christ*, R.J. Hollingdale, trans. (New York: Penguin Classics, 1968): 38

20. Our very human desire to hold a changing world steady in order to think and talk about it in language is, of course, connected to the problem of "reification," the thingification of abstract ideas. Marxist literature has explored extensively the political and economic consequences of the ways in which reification obscures, falsifies, and distorts social relationships, as in the problem of commodity fetishism, in which labor becomes a "thing" apart from and "against" the one who labors. See, e.g., Georg Lukács, *History and Class Consciousness* (Pontypool, Wales: Merlin Press, 1967) para. 66; and Fredric Jameson, "Reification and Utopia in Mass Culture," *Social Text* 1 (1979): 130-148.

Yet, the atemporality of nouns is misleading, even as to language itself. If we attend closely to our language practices, rather than our linguistic or grammatical categories, as Wittgenstein urged, we see that no such perduring "definition" binds things collected together under a noun as some kind of eternal Platonic Form; instead we see that the denotation and connotation of nouns change as contexts and analogies overlap (consider, for example, Wittgenstein's famous "what is a game?" thought experiment).[21] While grammar may not acknowledge it, language itself is temporal, enabling us to speak about new experiences through metaphor, poetry, and analogy rather than pigeonhole. Despite the hubris of a grammar that speaks in various tenses about past and future from a seemingly still point of present omniscience, we also know that language is always beholden to faulty memory, which fades and fools us. And, of course, even languages are born, change, and pass away.[22]

Like language, law can also be a kind of rebellion against finitude, as it reaches into the future with its "shalls" and "shall nots," promising commitment, connection, consistency, performance and punishment, and guaranteeing a stable, reliable future. But, like language, law—as both written rules and practices—also changes both suddenly and imperceptibly through context, application, and culture, and sometimes dies, is killed, or invisibly passes away.

The illusion of eternity—embedded, at least for language, in grammar—tricks us in our perception of time, as about many things. Time is the experience of the world from the point of view of a finite and changeable human mind, not an infinite yardstick available in an ev-

---

21. "Instead of producing something common to all that we call language, I am saying that these phenomena have no one thing in common which makes us use the same word for all,--but that they are *related* to one another in many different ways. And it is because of this relationship, or these relationships, that we call them all 'language.' ... Consider for example the proceedings that we call 'games.' I mean board-games, card-games, ball-games, Olympic games, and so on. What is common to them all? ... [I]f you look at them you will not see something that is common to *all*, but similarities, relationships, and a whole series of them at that." Ludwig Wittgenstein, *Philosophical Investigations*, trans. Gertrude E. M. Anscombe, third edition. (New York: Macmillan Company, 1958), at sections 65–66. See also sections 204 and 562–568.

22. More than 3,000 languages are expected to die before the end of the century. See Endangered Languages Project, www.endangeredlanguages.com

erlasting present to measure all of eternity. People do not remain the same, like nouns, over time. People grow and change and fade and die.

⊕

III. Doing x amount of time for x amount of crime

Modern sentencing practices, like our cosmological understanding of time, tend to treat time as number or as a presently-existing *quantity* of some *thing*. We easily speak of time as a "coin" in which to "repay" our "debt" to society. Plea-bargainers assess "what the case is worth" in months or years. Treating time as a quantity of some *thing* creates many conceptual miscues in the sentencing process.

First, the scalar nature of an infinite time-line tends to ignore the fact that human lives are not infinite, nor are they experienced evenly throughout. No one can serve three life sentences, 150 years or life plus 3,318 years.[23] Yet such sentences are not uncommon. Even if the purpose of such long sentences is to guarantee that you will not qualify for parole, these superhuman sentences may have anchoring effects in other cases that make a fifty-year sentence seem short by contrast, even though the experienced duration and actual service of such a sentence is likely to be the same whether it is fifty, a hundred, or a thousand years—i.e., the balance of the offender's life.[24] These numbers have meaning for us, in other words, not as durations but as quan-

---

23. For example, Clarence Aaron had been serving three life sentences since 1993 for conspiracy to distribute cocaine until the sentences were commuted by President Obama. See Cora Currier, "President Obama tells Clarence Aaron he can finally go home," ProPublica, Dec. 19, 2013; https://www.propublica.org/article/president-obama-tells-clarence-aaron-he-can-finally-go-home. Bernard Madoff was convicted of eleven federal felonies related to securities fraud and sentenced to 150 years. See Tomoeh Murakami Tse, "Madoff Sentenced to 150 Years," Washington Post, June 30, 2009; http://www.washingtonpost.com/wp-dyn/content/article/2009/06/29/AR2009062902015.html. James Eagan Holmes, who killed twelve people and wounded many others at a movie theater in Colorado, was sentenced to life plus 3,318 years. See Ann O'Neill, "Theater shooter Holmes gets 12 life sentences plus 3,318 years," CNN, August 27, 2015; http://www.cnn.com/2015/08/26/us/james-holmes-aurora-massacre-sentencing/index.html

24. Sentences longer than life also obscure the phenomenological difference between time experienced as a youth and time experienced as an older person. Time spent in prison when one is young is experienced as a greater percentage of one's life than time spent in prison when one is old.

tities. In federal sentencing practice, we further obscure the relation between sentences and human life by calculating and pronouncing guideline sentences in months rather than the familiar birthday-candle measure of years. One hundred and twenty months does not evoke the same associations as ten years, and we must translate from the abstract to the concrete everyday.

Second, the infinite "number-line" scalar conception of time tempts us to a matching scalar conception of "desert"—an imagined relationship between the nature and gravity of the offense and the "deserved" punishment. Where quantities are present in crimes in some way, we are tempted to establish a neat correspondence between a scalar factor in the crimes and our scalar idea of time. This is especially true when a crime involves money, perhaps because the "time is money, money is time" metaphor comes so easily to us.

In some sentencing contexts, the metaphoric relationship between time and money becomes literal: under the federal sentencing "loss" guidelines for fraud, for example, we key monetary loss directly to time in prison. These practices result in sentences that can far exceed a lifetime—as in Bernie Madoff's famous 150-year sentence. But unlike a debt or a mortgage, there is no way to make a balloon payment of time. We fail to take seriously those 150 years as a *duration* rather than an *amount*. The federal sentencing fraud "loss table" that exchanges months for dollars, as though they were merely a different form of currency, is reproduced in Table 1 (next page). [25]

Moreover, the financial loss incurred may in some fraud cases be less significant than other elements of desert. For example, stealing 40,000 dollars may involve years of lying to a series of trusting family friends; defrauding a series of lonely widows may involve a number of false marriage proposals. Such personal, calculated betrayals may be far more blameworthy, in terms of human suffering and *mens rea* callousness, than siphoning a million dollars in a single keystroke from

---

25. United States Sentencing Commission, *Guidelines Manual* (Washington, D.C.; November 2015), §2B1.1 (http://www.ussc.gov/sites/default/files/pdf/guidelines-manual/2015/2B1.1.pdf

Table 1:

Federal Sentencing Guidelines for "Basic Economic Offenses"
(larceny, embezzlement and other forms of theft) (U.S.S.G. 2B1.1)

§2B1.1. Larceny, Embezzlement, and Other Forms of Theft; Offenses Involving Stolen Property; Property Damage or Destruction; Fraud and Deceit; Forgery; Offenses Involving Altered or Counterfeit Instruments Other than Counterfeit Bearer Obligations of the United States

(a) Base Offense Level:

    (1) 7, if (A) the defendant was convicted of an offense referenced to this guideline; and (B) that offense of conviction has a statutory maximum term of imprisonment of 20 years or more; or

    (2) 6, otherwise.

(b) Specific Offense Characteristics

    (1) If the loss exceeded $6,500, increase the offense level as follows:

Loss	(Apply the Greatest)	Increase in Level
(A)	$6,500 or less	no increase
(B)	More than $6,500	add 2
(C)	More than $15,000	add 4
(D)	More than $40,000	add 6
(E)	More than $95,000	add 8
(F)	More than $150,000	add 10
(G)	More than $250,000	add 12
(H)	More than $550,000	add 14
(I)	More than $1,500,000	add 16
(J)	More than $3,500,000	add 18
(K)	More than $9,500,000	add 20
(L)	More than $25,000,000	add 22
(M)	More than $65,000,000	add 24
(N)	More than $150,000,000	add 26
(O)	More than $250,000,000	add 28
(P)	More than $550,000,000	add 30.

a hedge fund that barely registers the loss.[26] Yet, under the federal sentencing guidelines, sentencing has been far more heavily influenced

---

26. One famously skewed example is *United States v. Corsey*, 723 F.3d 366 (2d Cir. 2013). In that case, a trio of would-be fraudsters pretended to represent the long-defunct Yamasee Native American tribe, which was supposedly seeking to help the Buryatia people to build a pipeline across Siberia. The defendants sought to obtain a $3 billion loan from a financier, who was also an FBI informant, on the security of $5 billion in imaginary Treasury bills listed by number in an AOL email. The fraudsters promised the lender $14 billion in profit

by net loss than by "vulnerable victim" or "abuse of trust" sentencing enhancements. The quantifiable aspects of the crime seem somehow more objective and easier to set against a scale of time in prison, producing an illusion of symmetry between crime and time.[27]

Third, the equation of time and quantity (especially as money) gives support to the common but misleading metaphor of punishment as a debt-payment. Money, of course, is itself an abstraction. Money handily represents goods and services by how much people want them, in order to facilitate trades. In a familiar and neat feedback loop, the trades in turn determine *how* money measures the desire for goods and services. Time as wages, of course, also indirectly represents ser-

---

over five years. When asked if he wished to speak at sentencing, one of the defendants "launched into an impassioned account of the trials of the Yamasee tribe."

Based on the loss calculations for the "intended" fraud amount—3 billion dollars—the guideline ranges were "off the charts," and so each of the co-conspirators received the statutory maximum penalty of 20 years. Judge Stefan Underhill, concurring in the Second Circuit's remand for resentencing, argued that "the loss guideline is fundamentally flawed," because "the use of intended loss as a proxy for seriousness of the crime was wholly arbitrary," and the "farcical" negotiations resembled "a comedic plot outline for a 'Three Stooges' episode'" rather than a sophisticated fraud scheme. He thought the court should have overturned the sentence for substantive unreasonableness.

Recent amendments to the fraud guidelines have focused on redressing some of these concerns, especially as to expansive complicity rules and over-emphasis on total loss. See George Horn, "Sentencing Commission amends fraud guidelines," National Review, April 16, 2015 (quoting Commissioner Saris: "These amendments emphasize substantial financial harms to victims rather than simply the mere number of victims and recognize concerns regarding double-counting and over-emphasis on loss.")

27. In drug cases, we have chosen, somewhat arbitrarily, to key the calculus of desert not to the profits derived from the drug trade (as in fraud), but to the drug amounts sold. See United States Sentencing Commission, *Guidelines Manual*, at §2D1.1. Not only does this seem to be yet another way to disadvantage drug defendants vis-à-vis fraud defendants; further, under complicity and "relevant conduct" rules it makes the street dealers liable to the same penalties as the kingpins, because drug amounts are calculated for the conspiracy as a whole, regardless of the relative profits made by each defendant. Again, the adjustments to the sentence for "minimal participation" or "organizer" are minor compared to the weight given the quantifiable aspects of the crime, viz., the quantity of the contraband drug. While the monetizing of crime is not directly responsible for all of these built-in inequalities (complicity rules and a refusal to sentence by profit are also problematic), the sleight-of-hand that equates "time" with crime and treats both quantitatively, instead of qualitatively, helps to hide inequities. We see the satisfying scalar symmetry of the drug amount tables, and we fail to inquire further about whether the sentencing time really fits the crime.

vices and products (or power) of labor, though as Marx reminds us, in a highly alienated fashion.[28]

But time in prison represents the *absence* of goods and services—it is merely inactivity and non-production. So prison time is not like money at all. If anything, time in prison is more like accruing debt than paying it. And this idea of prison time as debt-accretion is no mere fiction in cases in which prisoners continue to accrue child support payments and court costs/fees/charges for and during their confinement.[29] If time in prison "pays back" for a crime somehow, it "pays back" in a way far more metaphorical than money does.

Fourth, the quantification and commodification of time allows the specious inference that we can "transfer" our time to others. This concept is also pernicious in the context of sentencing. We can act with or for others, and we can share the fruits of our activities with others; but we cannot "give" others our time, as such. Mortality is a fatal, non-exchangeable condition.

When we "do time" as punishment, we are not engaging in activities on behalf of others or sharing the fruits of those activities. What we are really doing is giving *up* activities or relationships. We "do" nothing when we merely "do" time, or, doing time is really a *not* doing time—a kind of prison as "opportunity cost." We must give up political action, friendship, work, service, family, friends, acquiring and possessing, artistic activity, creativity, exploration, travel, education, novel experience, and so forth.

The "opportunity cost" metaphor may be itself misleading, though. The idea of prison as "time" is not the same as the idea of prison as a "deprivation of freedoms." One may be deprived of some freedoms without being deprived of all agency and trajectory. Thinking of

---

28. In a pamphlet distributed in 1891, based on an earlier essay, Marx wrote: "He [the worker] does not even reckon labor as part of his life, it is rather a sacrifice of his life. It is a commodity which he has made over to another. Hence, also, the product of his activity is not the object of his activity.... On the contrary, life begins for him where this activity ceases...." Karl Marx, "Wage-Labor and Capital," in Robert C. Tucker, *The Marx–Engels Reader*, second edition (New York: W. W. Norton, 1978), 204–5.

29. See Pew Charitable Trusts, *Collateral Costs: Incarceration's Effect on Economic Mobility* (Philadelphia: Pew Charitable Trusts, 2010), based on research by Bruce Western and Becky Petit. http://www.pewtrusts.org/~/media/legacy/uploadedfiles/pcs_assets/2010/CollateralCosts1pdf.pdf

punishment *as* time, and only time, without more, is not punishment understood as the deprivation of certain freedoms, but punishment understood as a halt to human action and a deprivation of meaning.

Originally, of course, this stopping of action was meant to extract people from dangerous and destructive environments and to put them in quiet, safe, garden-like spaces, alone and undisturbed, where they would at last have time for contemplation, penitence, and reflection.[30] The ideal was to invite people in prison to reflect, meditate, pray or contemplate— forms of meaningful human action, not "mere time."[31] As instituted, however, the penitentiary became the notorious precursor of "mere time." The disappointed rant of reformer George Washington Smith, who had once advocated solitary confinement as a time for penitence and religious renewal, demonstrates the gulf between ideal and reality:

> No literary instruction whatever was imparted; the kind accents of mercy were never heard; the mild tones of persuasion, the language of earnest expostulation, were superseded by the more summary and more congenial measures of brutal violence. We are not therefore surprised that the perpetrators of the enormous outrages, these cool experimenters on the capabilities of human nature to endure excruciating, lingering suffering, deemed religious instruction not only unnecessary but pernicious! They ignorantly, presumptuously, impiously deemed, that the regenerating influence of religion was powerless within the walls of the purgatory they had instituted; that a class of men existed in whom hope and fear were alike extinct; to whom the threats of punishment or the hope of mercy ought not to be extended; and that such offenders whom the Almighty in his wisdom and his mercy still permitted to enjoy a period of further probation, were so incorrigible that every attempt should be made to prevent the possibility of their accepting the gracious offers of Providence.[32]

The "penitentiary" became the prison; prayerful time became *mere* time, stopping the possibility of all human action; and, like Oleson's punitive coma, excluding any purpose. To "do nothing" is to live

---

30. Adam J. Hirsch, *The Rise of the Penitentiary: Prisons and Punishment in Early America* (New Haven: Yale University Press, 1992).

31. See George W. Smith, *A Defence of the System of Solitary Confinement of Prisoners Adopted by the State of Pennsylvania, with remarks on the origin, progress and extension of this species of prison discipline* (Philadelphia: E.G. Dorsey / Philadelphia Society for Alleviating the Miseries of Public Prisons, 1833), 8–10. Reprint of the original essay published in the Philadelphia Gazette in 1828–29.

32. Ibid., 36-37.

without a sense of purpose, and, therefore, without the possibility of meaning. It is precisely not to "give our time to others." To "do time," then, is to live day to day *without* a justification, *without* a reason. So the ironic conundrum of time as punishment is this: How can there be a *justification* for the imposition of *meaninglessness?* Empty time as punishment is the imposition of "meaninglessness," hence it is difficult to see how this concept of "punishment as time" could be justified by a "rational basis" or a "penological objective." Time as punishment seems a contradiction in itself: Can the state have a purpose for eliminating purpose?[33] Can a "sentence" be gibberish?

IV. Is meaninglessness itself a kind of justified punishment?

The legal litany of the justifications for punishment is usually recited as: deterrence, incapacitation, retribution, and rehabilitation. I'll briefly consider each one.

Because a meaningless life is by definition not a desirable one, meaninglessness might be a candidate for a deterrent to crime. However, there is a trick here. Stilling human action does not create an "undesirable" condition, but a "desireless" condition—a condition of a lack of desire. In a condition of "lacking" desire, humans are not motivated at all, and the very human striving that is presupposed by deterrence theory is undermined. This is no mere philosophical deduction; the pervasive anomie in our prison system often leads to a listlessness in which those in prison "lose the ability to routinely initiate their own behavior or exercise sound judgment in making their own decisions …[they] may even become extremely uncomfortable and disoriented

---

33. Jonathan Goldberg-Hiller has already identified this contradiction: "In the context of punishment, we suggest, the difficulties of making coherent narrative identities and of construing a meaningful life within a remembered past and an active future are unaccounted aspects of punishment that expose more of its violence at the same time that they may frustrate some punitive goals." Goldberg-Hiller, "Time and Punishment," 627. In his notes, Goldberg-Hiller goes on to observe that "Ricoeur's perspective emphasizes the aporias between cosmological and phenomenological time, implicitly disturbing the assurance of the just measurement of punishment." He is here drawing on Ricoeur, *Time and Narrative*, vol. III, 12–96.

when and if previously cherished freedoms, autonomy, and choices are finally restored."[34]

Deterrence thinking may also create anomie because it "values" crime as a desirable activity that must be counterbalanced by a painful cost. It treats us all as willing law-breakers who are only restrained by the cost—calculated as the consequences multiplied by the probability of being caught, convicted, and sentenced. From such a perspective, punishments begin to look like mere prices in a marketplace.[35] Deterrence therefore undermines criminal law's moral legitimacy and, by some accounts, lessens the power of punishment to deter *by virtue of lessening its moral authority.*[36]

While confining those who may be dangerous may make the free members of society safer, meaningless time in confinement may serve to "incapacitate"—another often-cited purpose for punishment. But *meaningful* confinement would actually be safer, as prison officials find restive prisoners far more dangerous and much prefer that prisoners have something to do and something to care about. Former prison warden Dora Schriro argued for her "parallel universe" model of imprisonment, in which those in prison are given quasi-workplace incentives and goals that they help to design, in part on the ground that is it safer for everyone who works or lives inside the institution.[37]

In addition, the philosophical objections to both deterrence and incapacitation are well-rehearsed—both forms of penal justification are contrary to Kantian ideas of human dignity and autonomy that

---

34. Jeremy Travis and Michelle Waul, *Prisoners Once Removed: The Impact of Incarceration and Reentry on Children, Families, and Communities* (Washington, D.C.: Urban Institute, 2004): 40.

35. See, e.g., Linda Ross Meyer, "Herbert Morris and Punishment," *Quinnipiac Law Review* 22 (2003), 109.

36. Paul H. Robinson and John M. Darley, "The Utility of Desert," *Northwestern Law Review* 91 (1997), 453.

37. Dora Schriro, "How Arizona has created a parallel universe for inmates," *National Institute of Justice Journal* 263 (June 2009), 2–9. After Schriro initiated her new program, she reported that from 2004 to 2008 "inmate-on-inmate violence" decreased 46%, "inmate-on-staff" violence decreased 33%, suicide decreased 67%, and sexual assault decreased 61%. The parallel universe idea is not new. See Alexander Maconochie, *Crime and Punishment: The Mark System, framed to mix persuasion with punishment, and make their effect improving, yet their operation severe* (London: J. Hatchard and Son, 1846); accessed at https://babel. hathitrust.org/cgi/pt?id=nyp.33433075963326;view=1up;seq=5

require us to respect others for their intrinsic worth as persons, rather than manipulating them to our advantage. Both deterrence and incapacitation involve complicated economic calculations that interact oddly with the public sense of moral legitimacy—which itself creates a good deal of deterrence and incapacitation in the first instance.[38] The level of punishment that deters or incapacitates often does not jibe with the level of punishment that seems proportionate to the crime. Murder, to take the classic example, is often committed in situations of high emotional stress or fear, and is typically neither deterrable nor often repeated. Burglary, on the other hand, is in theory highly deterrable—yet strongly characterized by high rates of recidivism.[39] Even so, few would argue that burglary should be treated

---

38. See Neal Katyal, "Deterrence's Difficulty," *Michigan Law Review* 95 (1997), 2385. Katyal argues that casual references to deterrence fail to grasp the subtleties of substitution theory, and suggests that high penalties related to crack may drive drug markets to heroin—which is what seems to have happened. See also Robinson and Darley, "The Utility of Desert."

39. For one snapshot, see Department of Justice, Bureau of Statistics, *Recidivism of Prisoners Released in 30 States in 2005: Patterns from 2005 to 2011* (Washington, D.C.: Department of Justice, 2014), based on data analysis by Matthew R. Durose, Alexia D. Cooper, and Howard N. Snyder. Only 0.9% of all prisoners released are rearrested on homicide charges (Table 9, p. 9). Those previously in prison for murder had the lowest rates of rearrest: 10.1% had been rearrested for any offense after six months, 47.9% had another arrest for any offense after 5 years. Those released after burglary or larceny or weapons charges had the highest rates of rearrest for any offense: 31%, 39% and 35.3% respectively after six months and 81.8%, 84.1% and 79.5% respectively after five years (Table 8, p. 8). A similar disparity is evident if return to prison, rather than rearrest, is the measure of recidivism: After five years, 61.8% of property offenders returned to prison while 50.6% of violent offenders did so (Table 16, p. 15).

These statistics are difficult to interpret, however, because those released after sentences for murder are often older and for that reason may be less likely to resume criminal behavior. See Table 2, p. 3 (rearrest by age at release: 24 or younger, 78.2%, 40 or older, 62.9%). Those incarcerated for murder may also have fewer prior arrests, and for that reason be less likely to resume criminal behavior, as a longer criminal record also correlates with recidivism (p. 12). Those released after homicide charges have also generally received much longer sentences, so one might wonder whether the length of the sentence itself deters recidivism. While there is some correlation between longer sentences and lower recidivism (at least when compared to shorter carceral sentences, though not necessarily when compared to in-community sanctions), longer sentences have steeply diminishing returns. See, e.g., David S. Abrams, "How do we decide how long to incarcerate?" in Yun-chien Chang, ed., *Empirical Legal Analysis: Assessing the Performance of Legal Institutions* (New York: Routledge, 2014), 63–91.

According to the Bureau of Statistics analysis above, those previously convicted of violent crimes, while less likely to recidivate overall, are more likely to be re-arrested for violent crimes rather than property crimes in the future (33.1% of those re-arrested within

more harshly than homicide. For this reason, recent Supreme Court cases have shied away from justifying long sentences on deterrence or incapacitation grounds, and instead have required punishment to have a retributive or rehabilitative justification.[40]

Obviously, "meaningless" time does nothing to rehabilitate, if rehabilitation is thought to require some form of action during incarceration. Hence the most serious contender for a justification of meaningless confinement is retribution. Retribution aims at narrative equivalence between crime and punishment—a kind of fitting "just deserts" that reverses the direction of an actor's unethical conduct so that, in the classic retributive narrative, the offender suffers his own crime or, less figuratively and more philosophically, the offender is brought under the law of his own crime, universalized.[41]

Might our model of anomic sentencing be a kind of retributive equivalent to the state of "ethical loneliness" that the trauma of serious crime imposes on its victims? Jill Stauffer describes this condition of ethical loneliness, a term derived from philosopher and holocaust survivor Jean Améry, as "the phenomenological experience of having been abandoned by humanity."[42] Améry writes:

> SS-man Wajs from Antwerp, a repeated murderer and an especially adroit torturer, paid with his life. What more can my foul thirst for revenge demand? But if I have searched my mind properly, it is not a matter of re-

---

five years were arrested for violent crimes) than those previously convicted of property crimes (28.5% of those re-arrested within five years were arrested for violent crimes; Table 10, p. 9). This last difference, while statistically significant, was not especially dramatic. See Appendix, Table 11, p. 27 (standard error for violent/violent category was .57, standard error for property/violent category was .50).

Being black is also a significant predictor of being both a perpetrator and a victim of violence. "[P]eople sometimes kill simply to avoid being killed. As a result, disputes can escalate dramatically in environments (endogenously) perceived to be dangerous, resulting in self-fulfilling expectations of violence...and significant racial disparities in rates of murder and victimization." Brendan O'Flaherty & Rajiv Sethi, "Homicide in Black and White," *Journal of Urban Economics*, 68 (2010), 215:

40. General deterrence and incapacitation alone were insufficient to justify the penalties in *Panetti*, *Graham*, and *Miller*. See Dan Markel, "Executing Retributivism: The Future of the Eighth Amendment," *Northwestern University Law Review* 103 (2009), 1163.

41. See Michael S. Moore, "The Moral Worth of Retribution," in *Responsibility, Character and the Emotions*, ed. Ferdinand Schoeman, (New York: Cambridge University Press, 1987) 179-219.

42. Jill Stauffer, *Ethical Loneliness: The Injustice of Not Being Heard* (New York: Columbia University Press, 2015).

venge, nor one of atonement. The experience of persecution was, at the very bottom, that of an extreme loneliness. At stake for me is the release from the abandonment that has persisted from that time until today. When SS-man Wajs stood before the firing squad, he experienced the moral truth of his crimes. At that moment, he was with me—and I was no longer alone with the shovel handle. I would like to believe that at the instant of his execution he wanted exactly as much as I to turn back time, to undo what had been done. When they led him to the place of execution, the anti-man had once again become a fellow man.[43]

Both "doing time" and "ethical loneliness" are defined as living with a *lack* of law, a lack of justification, and a lack of community. So there is a kind of equivalence here between the suffering imposed at least on victims of serious violence and that suffered by prisoners "doing time." If Améry is correct, then the offender's experience of ethical loneliness is what can come to dispel it for the victim—the victim and offender are joined together in being separated from the world.

The problem is that the equivalence of "merely surviving without justification or purpose or community" is an equivalence that is already created in both offender and victim as a result of the crime itself. Georg Hegel, the nineteenth-century German philosopher, thought of the offender's deed as already having cast him or her outside of reason's bounds, to live in a kind of moral isolation from humanity. Crime, for Hegel, was a contradiction and a failure to universalize the maxim of one's action and to treat all reasonable creatures with consistency. Since crime makes an irrational exception of oneself, it is a repudiation of one's being as a human with reason and a form of self-exile. The idea of retributive punishment was to reverse that condition, not to manifest it further. By visiting the offender's own choices on herself, Hegel thought, punishment was not just the rebound of her crime, but a way to treat her, once again, as a reasonable being by including her in her own maxim and eliminating the inconsistency. Hegel conceived of retributive punishment as an offender's re-inclusion in the circle of humanity, through a participation in the universality of reason, not as a casting of the offender outside of reason and humanity altogether.

---

43. Jean Améry, *At the Mind's Limits: Contemplations by a Survivor on Auschwitz and its Realities*, Sidney Rosenfeld and Stella P. Rosenfeld, trans. (Bloomington, Ind.: Indiana University Press, 1980), 70.

To be cast out of the realm of reason was not punishment, but mere perishing.[44]

Hegel is echoed by Durkheim who, writing at the end of the nineteenth century, considered anomie as the reverse of punishment: Whereas punishment enacts and reinforces the social bond, anomie is a condition of social disintegration and a precondition for suicide.[45] Of Durkheim's account, Patricia Ewick has written:

> Durkheim offered a theory of punishment that recognized its religious quality and the degree to which the modern individual—elevated to the level of the sacred—lies at the heart of rituals of punishment. If punishment is to do its cultural work, it must express the distinction between "good" and "evil" by sacrificing the person to be punished. But in order for that to occur the creature must, paradoxically, be "worthy" of sacrifice, they must possess a self. If it is to be legitimate — that is, if it is to be meaningful — punishment must paradoxically sustain the punished as sacred, as human, even while it seeks to degrade and condemn them. To fail in this regard, that is to profane that which is not sacred, is a semiotically futile gesture.[46]

A comprehensive study of custodial suicides produced in 2010 by the National Institute of Corrections documented a suicide rate between three and six times higher in prisons than among the general population.[47] While it is the case that increased vigilance and improved

---

44. Georg Hegel, *Elements of the Philosophy of Right*, Allen W. Wood, ed., trans. H. B. Nisbet (Cambridge: Cambridge University Press, 1991), 119–131. For a discussion of Hegel's theory, see Linda R. Meyer, *The Justice of Mercy* (Ann Arbor, Mich.: University of Michigan Press, 2010), chapter 4.

45. Emile Durkheim, *Suicide: A Study in Sociology*, George Simpson, ed., trans. John A. Spaulding and George Simpson (New York: Free Press, 1951), esp. chapter 5. Simon Critchley offers a contrasting view:

> Why not attempt a minimal conversion away from the self-aversion that lacerates and paralyzes us towards another possible version of ourselves? Is this not finally more courageous? Such is perhaps what Nietzsche calls the pessimism of strength as opposed to an optimism of naivety and weakness. True pessimists don't kill themselves.… If we cannot find reasons to be, then perhaps it is better not to be. But that would be a huge mistake, a fatal misstep. The question of life's meaning is an error and should simply be given up. The great revelation will never come.… Instead…there are little daily miracles, matches struck in the dark.

Simon Critchley, *Notes on Suicide* (London: Fitzcarraldo Editions, 2015), 73, 75–6.

46. See Patricia Ewick, "The Return of Restraint: Limits to the Punishing State," *Quinnipiac Law Review* 31 (2013), 596–7.

47. U.S. Department of Justice, National Institute of Corrections, *National Study of Jail Suicide: 20 Years Later*, Lindsay M. Hayes, Project Director (Washington: U.S. Department of Justice, April 2010), NIC Accession No. 024308.

monitoring systems have reduced the number of successful suicides in custody, attempted suicides are still common.[48]

The punishment of "doing time" does nothing to heal or change the condition of ethical loneliness for either the defendant or the victim; it merely imposes a second dose of ethical loneliness on the offender to be "even," deepening the ethical loneliness rather than alleviating it.

But Améry demands more than a merely conceptual loneliness that an offender suffers by doing an act contrary to reason; he demands as well that the offender *experience* absolute abandonment. Only then, he believes, will the offender "revolt against reality, which [reality] is rational only as long as it is moral. The moral person demands the annulment of time…by nailing the criminal to his deed. Thereby, and through a moral turning back of the clock, the latter can join his victim as a fellow human being."[49]

The desperate demand for a return of a "moral reality," Améry believes, can only come to the offender *through* the experience of moral abandonment, and perhaps only through a confrontation with death, at the moment before death. To extend Améry's argument to "doing time" (perhaps improperly), the experience of enduring "mere time," which creates anomie in the offender, awakens her desire and demand for what is missing (meaning, reason and community) and therefore she repudiates the crime. This desire to step out of an anomic loneliness is not just a precondition of a renewed bond with the victim, but—in Améry's language—the shared experience of loneliness also *is* the bond with the victim.

Such anomic punishment is not unknown. In the early to mid-nineteenth century, hard labor often consisted of punishments like the crank and the shot-drill, precisely designed to require painful, repetitive effort in order to perform utterly useless tasks. The crank, as its name suggests, was a machine that consisted of a crank, a counter that recorded the number of revolutions, and a screw mechanism that could be adjusted by the jailer to make the turning of the crank more

---

48. Anasseril E. Daniel, "Preventing Suicide in Prison: A Collaborative Responsibility of Administrative, Custodial, and Clinical Staff," *Journal of the American Academy of Psychiatry and the Law* 34 (June 2006) 165–75.

49. Améry, *At the Mind's Limits*, 72.

or less difficult. One would be required to perform thousands of revolutions of this crank in one's cell each day in order to qualify for meals of more than bread and water. The shot drill consisted of the pointless moving of 32-pound cannon shot three to five steps over, and then back again. One could not bend one's knees or make any noise during this procedure, in order "to increase the severity of the punishment."[50] The Sisyphean hopelessness induced by such punishments was meant to break the will of the prisoner, inducing despair, and thereafter, an abject submission and repentance.

If such anomic forms of "doing time" could necessarily evoke such an experience of ethical loneliness that called attention to "the wrong as wrong,"[51] then perhaps time itself could be the ground of the reunification that retribution seeks, and "doing time" would have its retributive justification. But it is a fallacy to believe, I think, that any particular form of violence can swerve a soul toward repentance rather than a new resentment. "Doing time" may be meaningless and lonely, but there is by definition also and, ironically, no meaning in "mere time" that ties such suffering to the crime or the victim. "Doing time" forgets relationships and forges emptiness; however acute the suffering, it does not necessarily call to mind the crime or remembrance of the victim.

I once asked my imprisoned students if they would be interested in having a chance to apologize to their victims. I was surprised by the response; several burst into tears of remorse. But when the conversation centers on the particular length of their sentences, they often react with resentment—they experience their treatment by the criminal justice system as disconnected from their crimes, a disconnect that is, in the Connecticut state system, perhaps exacerbated by a plea bargain system in which deals are struck by judges, defense attorneys, and prosecutors with neither the participation of, nor any explanation to, the defendants. Each sentence number emerges mysteriously from behind closed doors and, once prisoners compare their numbers with

---

50. "Life in a Military Prison," *The Cornhill Magazine* 15:88 (April, 1867), 499–512, esp. 509ff. Accessed at https://babel.hathitrust.org/cgi/ pt?id=hvd.32044092653302;view=2up;seq=556

51. Meyer, *The Justice of Mercy*, 87–8.

each other, the differences between them seem inexplicable and meaningless. The meaninglessness of the numbers seems, anecdotally at least, to cause more resentment than remorse.

If temporality is the condition of a meaningful human life, "doing time" is, quite simply, inhuman.[52] Both ethical loneliness and doing "mere time" are denials of humanity, a murder of personhood. Perhaps we might also characterize "doing time" as a state of enforced anomic persistence (or, perhaps, "bare life"), the very antithesis of the pursuit of happiness. We might imagine claiming for both victim and prisoner a natural right to exist *in time*, with projects, actions, and plans.[53]

V. Bad Time and Good Time

How do we think of human life as purposeful? We should remember that there are many different traditions and understandings of a meaningful life, among them, for example:

- Productivity—achieving, building, learning, or creating something, either alone or as part of a team.
- Struggle and overcoming—a heroic story or political narrative of overcoming obstacles: leaving, learning, and a wiser returning; union and reunion; redemption; helping others overcome obstacles.

---

52. Jennifer Culbert explores Hannah Arendt's views on punishment, expressed in *Eichmann in Jerusalem: a Report on the Banality of Evil*, noting that for Arendt:

[O]nly in the presence of others do individual human beings appear and act as such. … human beings are distinguished from other forms of life by the fact that they can act, in speech and deed, to bring new things or states of being into the world. For these acts to take place or become real, other human beings must acknowledge and remember them. To be deprived of this space and the presence of others is to be deprived of the condition that confers reality on the founding and preservation of something new. In other words, to be deprived of this space and the presence of others is to be deprived of the condition that permits human beings to be distinctly human."

Jennifer Culbert, "The Banality of Death in *Eichmann in Jerusalem*," *Theory & Event* 6:1 (2002); DOI 10.1353/tae.2002.0004.

53. See Brian Orend, *Human Rights: Concept and Context* (Peterborough, Ont.: Broadview Press, 2002) 47, explicating Alan Gewirth's idea that the human capacity for practical wisdom is core and requires opportunity for action, as well as the means.

- Participation—fulfilling a social role in "the circle" of life or nature, moving from child to parent to grandparent, from birth to death, in solidarity and communion with others.
- Seeking or achieving union with one's God.
- Learning as an end in itself.
- Creating as an end in itself.
- Ethical action or virtue as an end in itself.
- Loving others as an end in itself.

Just "doing time" is none of these. Indeed, a key insight of nearly every Western ethical theory is that activity is central to human satisfaction. Robert Nozick famously imagined an "experience machine" that allows us to "feel" pleasure or have vicarious experience. Nozick concluded that such a machine would not constitute a satisfying substitute for activity with consequences in the world.[54] Martha Nussbaum's capabilities approach and John Finnis's natural rights theory, for all their ideological differences, reach similar conclusions.[55] And of course Aristotle understood that virtue was an "activity of the soul" that was dormant during sleep.[56]

Of course, in prison, no one (except perhaps those in solitary confinement) actually "just does time." Like weeds in the cracks of a sidewalk, people create worlds and villages and selves, even under prison conditions. Any prison memoir or testimony reveals the importance of relationships in prison, however we may discourage them. Even on death rows, where interactions are most sparse, friendship happens.[57] And despite uniforms and uniformity, expressions of individuality and

---

54. Robert Nozick, *Anarchy, State, and Utopia* (New York: Basic Books, 1974).

55. Martha Nussbaum, "Capabilities and Human Rights," *Fordham Law Review* 66(1997), 273; John Finnis, *Natural Law and Natural Rights*, second edition (Oxford: Oxford University Press, 2011).

56. Aristotle, *Nicomachean Ethics*, ed. and trans. Roger Crisp (Cambridge: Cambridge University Press, 2000), I.13.

57. See Joseph M. Giarrantano, "The Pains of Life," in *Facing the Death Penalty: Essays on a Cruel and Unusual Punishment*, ed. Michael L. Radelet (Philadelphia, Penn.: Temple University Press, 1989) 194–5, recounting a painful farewell by telephone with his prison-mentor and friend Mike, who was about to be executed:

"I love you, my friend. I'm sorry I can't stop this." Mike's reply still rings in my ear: "I'll be fine, Joe. You know that I'm going home. Please don't do anything you might regret later. You have to forgive them."

creativity emerge—hairstyles, make-up, tattoos, subtle clothing alterations, and the like. The problem is that the *idea* of "just doing time" creates institutions *designed* to pave over as much human soil as possible. Made in the image of "just doing time," we often design prisons and prison policy to cut off and frustrate most forms of meaningful human action.

In many prison settings, there is little support for finding meaning in productivity, creativity, or in the achievement of goals. In most prisons, programming is limited, difficult to access, and the first thing to fall to budget cuts. Nor can one usually keep or profit from one's creative activities. For example, I've seen women crocheting in prison like Odysseus's wife Penelope in Homer's *Odyssey*, constantly undoing and reworking their projects because they are not allowed to keep the finished articles.

One cannot "overcome" narrative obstacles in prison, because every day one faces, like Sisyphus, the eternal return of the very same obstacles—repetitive cleaning tasks, crude and offensive comments, often pointless regimentation. "How can we grow up in here," one young woman asked me, "if we never experience anything and nothing ever changes?"

One is hindered in building meaningful relationships because one's living situation is frequently shifted; talking and socializing is discouraged or heavily restricted; and guards are changed every few weeks or months precisely to *avoid* developing meaningful relationships. Visiting with family is hindered by artificially expensive phone services, lack of public transportation, artificial and highly restricted conditions for visits (even with children) and restricted hours for calls and contacts.[58]

---

58. See N. G. La Vigne, "Examining the effect of incarceration and in-prison family contact on prisoners' family relationships," *Journal of Contemporary Criminal Justice* 21 (Nov. 2005), 314; and U.S. Bureau of Justice Statistics, "Parents in prison and their minor children," August 30, 2008. In October 2015, the Federal Communications Commission capped rates for local and in-state long-distance calling for those in prison and cut the existing cap on interstate long-distance rates. The new rules were scheduled to take effect in June of 2016, but were partially stayed by the D.C. Circuit pending review in Global Tel*Link v. F.C.C., No. 15-1461, after being challenged by phone companies and the states that receive commissions from them. www.fcc.gov/consumers/guides/inmate-telephone-service.

One may of course still find meaning in religion, and many do, but even a meditative or contemplative approach to meaningful life is hindered by the constant noise and lack of privacy inherent in over-crowded prison conditions. Any still, small voices that might offer themselves are all but drowned out.[59]

Even though prisons are designed in many ways to frustrate meaningful action, most prison administrators don't see their mission as forcing prisoners to merely "do time," except, perhaps, in the horrific context of solitary confinement.[60] On the contrary, prison administrators—out of concern for prison and community safety and basic humanity (and, even more optimistically, to enhance people's chances of success after prison)—try to come up with "programming" (if they can afford it) to fill the swaths of empty time and make imprisonment at least *seem* to have a meaningful trajectory and a narrative arc.[61] If the dominant rhetoric at sentencing is about retribution and the *quantitative* fit between the crime and the time, the dominant narrative inside prison is about therapy and atonement, and the *qualities* of change and rehabilitation.

So, though judges and legislators naturally employ the (eternalizing) scalar rhetoric of proportionality and retribution, prisons naturally employ the (temporal) narrative rhetoric of rehabilitation, self-improvement, and redemption. The ideal and goal of punishment is, hence, understood dramatically differently in the courtroom—whether the sentencing scheme is indeterminate (as in Connecticut)

---

59. Even if prisons retained their original justification as places for penitence, obviously it would be difficult to justify prison in today's secular state on the sole ground that it encourages religious life.

60. There is ample and important literature on the experience of solitary confinement. Excellent and evocative writing on this topic includes: Goldberg-Hiller, "Time and Punishment," at 650ff; Caleb Smith, The Prison and the American Imagination (New Haven, Conn.: Yale University Press, 2009); Colin Dayan, The Law is a White Dog (Princeton, N.J.: Princeton University Press, 2008); Lisa Guenther, Solitary Confinement: Social Death and Its Afterlives (Minneapolis, Minn.: University of Minnesota Press, 2013).

61. The U.S. National Institute of Corrections has many resources on "best practices" that focus heavily on individual needs assessments and "individual development plans." See NCIC annotated bibliography of "what works:" https://s3.amazonaws.com/static.nicic.gov/Library/026917.pdf.

or highly regulated by rules (as in federal court)—and in the warden's office.

Compare the following transcripts of sentencing practices in Connecticut state court and federal court with the approach to serving time as described in the Connecticut Department of Correction's *Accountability Plan*:

A. Connecticut State Court

"THE DEFENDANT: I'm ready to plead. I'm ready to plead. I just need a couple of weeks so I could prepare myself to come in.

THE COURT: No.

THE DEFENDANT: I'm ready to plead. I'm not—

THE COURT: Listen. Here—

THE DEFENDANT: I'm going in blinded, broke—

THE COURT: Hold on. Just a second. Okay. You had alternate offers coming in to today. You're scheduled for a violation of probation hearing today which means depending upon the outcome of the violation of probation you could have been incarcerated as of five o-clock tonight for four and a half years. That was the possibility. Your attorney argued very eloquently for you in there and got me to reduce your prison term for today with the understanding that you were going in today. Now if you say I'm going to plead, I'll take that deal and be here tomorrow to go in, that's fine. If you're saying to me, I'm not going to do it because I want two weeks then it goes back to 15-7-3, which is 84 months in prison … rather than 66 months in prison…. So you tell your lawyer what you want to do because if you don't want the offer as it stands today then at 2 o'clock we may or may not be starting a violation of probation hearing on you and the whole deal is off. The State wanted 20 years. All right?… For one moment and one moment I have a little bit of a weakness to give you 15 after 66 months. Either you want it or you don't."[62]

B. Federal Sentencing Transcript

I will now state on the record the specific reasons for imposing the sentence I have just imposed.

As to the term of incarceration, the guideline range is 78 to 97 months. I have made a substantial downward departure and have imposed a term of 24 months' incarceration as to each count, with that sentence to run concurrent as to each count. I believe this sentence does adequately address the sentencing objectives of punishment and deterrence, and I will state on the record the reasons for making my downward departure in just a minute.

---

62. *State of Connecticut v. Davis* (transcript on file with author).

The order of restitution and fine are made for the reason I believe that, under the record before me, such restitution and fine are justified and do meet the ends of justice in this case.

The supervised release is imposed for the reason I believe the defendant will need this amount of supervision to see that he reassimilates himself back in society, that he obtains suitable employment, that he maintains a law-abiding life-style, that he pays the restitution and the fine.

The special assessment of $4,700 is imposed because the law mandates that it be imposed. That's $100 as to each count of conviction.

I will now state on the record the reasons for making the downward departure that I have just made.

Very few cases brought before this court have the potential to impact not only science, education, medicine, and research, but society as a whole by the restrictions and limitations placed on the transportation of hazardous and biological material as they relate to medical and academic research.

This court in no fashion condones the actions taken by the defendant in his illegal transportation of yersinia pestis to Tanzania. However, the court is of the opinion that while the defendant's actions are covered by Section 2M5.1 of the guidelines, mitigating circumstances exist to such a degree that the court does not believe a base offense level of 26 adequately achieves the desired outcome of the United States Sentencing Commission in their formulation of the United States Sentencing Guidelines. As a result, the court considers that the defendant's conduct regarding his conviction for unauthorized export to Tanzania is outside the heartland of the guidelines as noted in Section 5K2.0 and the application notes to the guidelines, Section 2M5.1, and therefore, I have assessed a downward departure.[63]

C. Description of Connecticut's Offender Accountability Plan (often required of each new prisoner upon entry into prison)

A. INTRODUCTION

An Offender Accountability Plan (OAP) shall be developed for each fully sentenced offender, formulating treatment goals and programming needs. The OAP is a tool designed to identify and address specific areas that need to be modified in order to assist the offender in a successful reintegration into the community. The foundation of the OAP is accountability, with each individual accepting responsibility to engage in productive endeavors.

Each offender's OAP shall be reviewed, and when necessary modified, on a regular basis throughout the term of incarceration in order to assess progress and reinforce achievement of stated goals. In addition to participation in identified treatment, educational and vocational programs, the OAP addresses safety and security issues, to include behavioral expectations (i.e. disciplinary reports, etc.).

---

63. *U.S. v. Butler* (N.D. Texas 2004) https://fas.org/butler/sentence.html

The final phase of the OAP prepares the offender for transition into the community, either by way of supervised community release or full discharge from their sentence. [64]

In the state court transcript, the defendant is faced with a sentence that appears almost meaningless and is deeply inflected by *the time he is saving the court*, rather than the time that fits the crime. Of course, defense lawyers, prosecutors, and judges will determine behind closed doors "what the case is worth" based on many other factors as well, including the nature of the crime, the mitigating circumstances, the defendant's prospects for rejoining the community, remorse, and the strength of the evidence. Many defense lawyers argue that the number that ultimately arrives in the public courtroom is a kind of tailored, individualized justice. But it is also mostly unexplained, secret, and approached as a debt paid primarily in the coin of time, in which a "program sentence" is a rare win for defense counsel, rather than a default option.

In federal court, the quantitative, time-frozen, and retributive approach to sentencing inside the courthouse necessarily jars with the rehabilitative and temporal understanding that is at least intoned if not supported by programming inside the prison. No matter what an offender does inside to atone or change, the retributive sentence remains the same, "freeze-framed" in the past and calibrated, like money, according to some quasi-monetized gain/loss/damage.

Only after sentencing is any mention made of what an offender will actually do once arriving at prison. And if he is to do "nothing," then he might indeed prefer a punitive coma—or might simply try to make life as difficult for his jailors as possible, out of sheer boredom and a desire not to become invisible. Hence, provision for some form of "good time" sentence credit becomes almost a necessity in a prison system in order to bring prisoners a sense of progress,[65] i.e., "exis-

---

64. State of Connecticut Offender Accountability Plan; http://www.ct.gov/doc/lib/doc/pdf/offenderaccountabilityplan.pdf

65. See Alison Lawrence, "Cutting Correction Costs: Earned Time Policies for State Prisoners," (Denver, Colo.: National Conference of State Legislatures, 2009); accessed at http://www.ncsl.org/Portals/1/Documents/cj/Earned_time_report.pdf

tence" (in Heidegger's sense), and of living *in* time rather than persisting "like a rock beside the road."[66]

One famous example of the tension between rhetorical discussions of retribution and rehabilitation is the many parole attempts of Leslie Van Houten. A Charles Manson follower who participated in two murders, Van Houten was sentenced in 1969, and she has come up for parole in California twenty times. She has earned two college degrees, aided elderly inmates, mentored, served, and accumulated a host of certificates and accolades for work in prison. At her twentieth parole hearing in 2013, these accomplishments were noted by the panel that finally recommended her for consideration for parole—only to have that recommendation rejected by a legal panel of the California Board of Parole Hearings. Nearly every news account lingered on the lurid details of the Manson Family's crimes, published old photographs of Van Houten at age 22—and paid little attention to the details of Van Houten's constructive work inside the prison. Van Houten testified, "I know I did something that is unforgiveable, but I can create a world where I make amends. I'm trying to be someone who lives a life for healing rather than destruction."[67] Again this year, just as this book goes to press, in her twenty-first appearance before a panel weighing her past and determining her future, Van Houten has received a recommendation to be approved for parole. Whether this recommendation will be accepted by the two steps of review imposed by California law—first a legal review by the Board of Parole Hearings, and finally a decision by the governor—remains to be seen.[68]

66. Natalie Babbitt, *Tuck Everlasting* (New York: Farrar, Straus and Giroux, 1975, 2000).

67. Associated Press, "Parole Denial for Leslie Van Houten suggests stigma too great for release of Manson followers," June 6, 2013; accessed at http://www.foxnews.com/us/2013/06/06/parole-denial-for-leslie-van-houten-suggests-stigma-too-great-for-release.html

68. http://www.npr.org/sections/thetwo-way/2016/04/15/474345032/california-panel-recommends-parole-for-former-manson-follower-leslie-van-houten

VI. Alternative: "Serving" a sentence: Sentencing as service

Why not unify these two rhetorics? Why not acknowledge temporality and change and allow up-front a narrative, atonement approach to sentencing? Why not connect the thought-silos of the sentencing hearing and the prison? Can sentencing be perceived *from the outset* as redemptive action rather than "time deservedly served?"[69]

Imagine the following sentencing hearings, expressing three different understandings of the same three-year time period:

1. Time is considered as a commodified abstraction, punishment as impersonal retributive equivalence between crime and sentence:

"You have pled guilty to 21 USC 841. Based on the amount of drugs involved in your conspiracy as a whole, your base offense level is 24, and that's a plus 2 because you obstructed justice by leaving the country, and a minus 4 because you were a minimal participant. You also get a minus 3 for pleading guilty and accepting responsibility. You have waived your right to appeal the sentence. So that's a level 19, and it puts you at 30-37 months for a criminal history score of 1. I'm sentencing you to 36 months."

2. Sentenced time is acknowledged as non-fungible and part of a human life experience, but punishment is still "mere time," imagined as retributive and meaningless:

"I sentence you to three years. During this time you will spend every holiday away from your loved ones, even as your children grow up and your parents die. It will be difficult for anyone to visit you, because you will serve your sentence in a state three thousand miles away from your home.

---

69. This idea is not, of course, a novel one. In 1846, Alexander Maconochie, prison warden and reformer in Australia, who is known as the "father of parole," wrote: "Slavery deteriorates;—long seclusion deteriorates;—every condition, in a word, more or less deteriorates, which leaves no choice of action…. What improves, on the contrary, is a condition of adversity from which there is no escape but by continuous effort—which leaves the degree of that effort much in the individual's own power…. [W]ere our sentences measured by labor instead of by time—were they the performance of certain tasks, not to the occupation of a certain time in evading any,—the approximation [to a condition which improves] might be made indefinitely close…. We become indifferent in spite of ourselves when engaged in a hopeless task." Maconochie, *Crime and Punishment: The Mark System*, 43–4, 46.

I further sentence you to change your abode and your living partner every six weeks and to adjust to a new authority figure every eight weeks in order to be sure that you form no solid expectations, routines, or new friendships, until you have forgotten how to care and connect with others. I sentence you to spend these years without having any new experiences. I sentence you to have very little control over your body or your health or your food. I sentence you to see those who love you gradually fade from your life, until you have little to say to them and they have little in common with you.[70] I sentence you to miss the opportunity to rock your baby to sleep, to miss your daughter's graduation and your son's wedding. I sentence you to lose your career dreams and sense of mission in the world. Know that you will also probably not find a job when you get out. I sentence you to know your children, parents, and friends are in pain, without your being able to help or comfort them. I sentence you to watch those around you go home while you have to remain behind. I sentence you to constantly adjust to living with people you do not like and who do not like you. I sentence you to a legal hell of hopes raised and dashed. I sentence you to emotional deprivation, repression and boredom, until you find yourself unable to feel and unable to choose. I sentence you to meaningless labor, to constant humiliation and disrespect, to tasteless and dangerous food and ugly surroundings, to extreme poverty of opportunities and possessions, to no control over the tangible productions of your creativity and imagination, to no peace, no quiet, no personal space, and no privacy, to days and nights that are exactly the same for years except for occasional random acts of violence and pervasive fear. I sentence you to form no relationships, to have no settled expectations, to form no projects for the future, to make no sense of your life."[71]

3. Sentenced time is understood as meaningful action toward atonement.

"James, you are sentenced to no more than three years, during which time you will have the opportunity to take responsibility for your criminal conduct. (If you maintain your innocence, you will, of course, have access to the courts to contest your conviction.) You will also get the chance to talk to the sentencing judge once a month to report on your progress and let the judge know if you have any concerns. If you complete the sentencing tasks early, you may be released early from state supervision. We will support you

---

70. Said Sayrafiezadeh, "Remembering My Mother's Obsession," *New York Times*, January 29, 2014; http://opinionator.blogs.nytimes.com/2014/01/29/meetings-with-a-murderer/?ref=opinion

71. For some examples of how meaningless time is experienced, see Shane Bauer, "Solitary in Iraq Nearly Broke Me: Then I Went Inside America's Prisons," *Mother Jones*, November–December 2012. http://www.motherjones.com/politics/2012/10/solitary-confinement-shane-bauer; John Eligon, "Two Decades in Solitary," *New York Times*, September 23, 2008, http://www.nytimes.com/2008/09/23/nyregion/23inmate.html?pagewanted=all; and "Voices From Solitary," Solitary Watch Blog, March 11, 2013, http://solitarywatch.com/2013/03/11/voices-from-solitary-a-sentence-worse-than-death/

as much as we can, and we know you can succeed, but you have work to do in order to turn your life around.

"The first thing is that we want you to have the chance to come to terms with your crime. Generally, but not always, this requires a period of time spent in a calmer place, separate from the situations and people and context of your crime.[72] Otherwise, it's just too difficult both for you to get reflective distance on what happened, and, if your crime endangered others, for those around you to feel safe again. It also may be that you are still a serious danger to yourself or others, and for that reason, you cannot return to your regular life right away.

"We think that part of this exploration of the past should involve a confrontation with the real ways your actions hurt people. You may not see it this way, but you need to at least listen to the perspectives of those you injured, even if you don't agree with them. You can do this perhaps by working with former offenders, or through conversations with your victims or with people who have been hurt by crimes like yours. You may also have the chance to offer a confidential apology, if your victim is willing to hear it. The goal of this first stage of the sentence is to understand the past—what your crime meant, what suffering and consequences it entailed, and how it is that you came to commit it, including figuring out what steps you might take to avoid harming others in the future.

"There are a lot of people who have been through this before and who are now going to lend a hand to help you through. They have helped each other think through and manage the circumstances that contributed to hurting other people, and you can talk with them about their experiences. Depending on what you, your family, and your support groups come up with, we can provide support for, for example, helping you get away from harmful addictions, getting you health care, and/or getting you help talking through violence or depression you suffered, which made you (perhaps rightly) angry and resentful, is holding you back, getting you into trouble, or making it all too easy to hurt others. Your children or family will also be able to visit you, receive family therapy if they desire, and strengthen their ties with you, if that seems likely to be good for you and for them, through visitation and special programming. We will also do our best to support them financially, if necessary, to ensure that your family remains strong while you are not with them.

"Then, when you complete your assessment of the past, we want you to have the chance to do something noble that will also help others trust you

---

72. For example, if the defendant has been out on bail, offenseless, and employed for a long period of time before sentencing, there seems no reason to require a period of incarceration that would only disrupt progress already made. (That doesn't mean that the defendant shouldn't tender some service, just that the "service" shouldn't be time.) Unfortunately, the intervals of time between crime, indictment and sentencing, especially in federal court, mean that many defendants are incarcerated after they have already stopped their criminal conduct and changed their lives.

again. We will offer you a choice of opportunities for meaningful community service, as a way for you to express remorse, reconnect with others, and/or demonstrate solidarity with your community: e.g., fire-fighting, nurse-assistant training, trail maintenance, service-dog training, caring for those in need, or providing emergency assistance around the world. This service may be in your own community, or it may be in a different place, depending on what options fit your goals and what seems best for regaining trust and acceptance in your community. Sometimes more time is needed away from home in order to change old patterns or to enable community members to heal and regain trust in you. We hope that this decision would be based in part on your thoughts and on the thoughts of members of your family, neighborhood, and community. Again, the hope would be that you will be able to give back to the people you've hurt and to your community, forge new sustaining relationships through teamwork, atone for your wrong, feel proud of your service instead of shamed by your crime or conviction, and that you and those you come to work with will be able to help each other maintain a safe, stable, meaningful, and crime-free life after your return home. What you do, and how much time you spend serving in this way should come in the form of a mediated or arbitrated settlement, determined by you, your attorney, your family, your victims, your judge, experienced ex-offenders and counselors, and by the nature and difficulty of the service itself.

"After completing intensive, meaningful, and responsible service, you will have the opportunity, if you want it, and it seems to fit your situation, to gain training for a new future. You may want to spend time achieving a GED, an associate's degree, or receiving vocational training or retraining in a field in which there are job opportunities in your community. We will also make available job sites where you can practice what you've learned and gain respect, trust, and experience. When you return to regular life, we want you to have the skills you need to support yourself and your family, contribute to your community, and recompense your victim. We also want to make sure that you have work and goals that make you strong and proud. During this period, you may spend time transitioning back home more slowly (if you have not already rejoined your community), so that you aren't overloaded with family and work responsibilities all at once. You may, for example, live for a while in a half-way house near your family where some of the burden of finding food, shelter, and support is eased. That way you'll have time to find work, figure out health care, work through complicated family relationships, and develop good support groups.[73] Throughout

---

73. See, for example, Tracy Connor, "Firefighting Felons: Hundreds of Inmates Battling the Yosemite Blaze," NBC News, August 30, 2013 (http://www.nbcnews.com/news/us-news/firefighting-felons-hundreds-inmates-battling-yosemite-blaze-v20232116)Celeste Fremon, "Firefighters Arnie Quinones & Ted Hall: A Hero Story," *Witness LA*, August 31, 2009 (http://witnessla.com/fire/2009/admin/firefighters-arnie-quinones-ted-hall-a-hero-story/); and Recidivism Reduction Committee of the Connecticut Sentencing Commission,

this process, you'll have the chance to check in with your sentencing judge, report on your progress, and ask for any support you need. After a successful transition, you will be invited and expected, if your circumstances allow, to help mentor others who are working toward atonement, just as you were helped."

$$\bigoplus$$

VII. Objections and Responses

The most idealistic visions of prison reform in the past have often produced the most inhumane prison conditions. Solitary confinement was originally meant to provide peaceful contemplation and facilitate self-reflection and religious conversion; imprisonment at hard labor was originally meant to provide a sense of autonomy and accomplishment, and offer a means of physical fitness.[74] Reformers often fail to acknowledge their own temporality, presuming to have an absolute answer for all time. Hence, I add the following set of objections and possible responses, both to acknowledge the problems with the model I set out above, and to suggest that readers retain a wariness about every project for reform—including this one.

Objection 1: Indeterminate Sentencing, Redux

The most persistent problem with sentencing as service instead of time is that we want there to be an "end" of the sentence and not a kind of endless supervision and thought-control, with prisoners abjectly begging to all-powerful parole authorities that they have "reformed." The most common abuses of modern indeterminate sentencing are illustrated by the Van Houten case; freedom is dangled before the pris-

---

Evidence-Based Reentry Initiatives Devoted to Strengthening Positive Social Relationships, Draft Report, September 20, 2012. (http://www.ct.gov/opm/lib/opm/cjppd/cjabout/ sentencingcommission/20120920_recidivism_reduction_strengthening_positive_social_ relationships.pdf). A significant relevant court case is *Pepper v. United States,* 131 S. Ct. 1229 (2011), which allows consideration of post-sentence rehabilitation under the federal sentencing guidelines sentencing practice. See also Jonathan Simon, *Poor Discipline: Parole and the Social Control of the Underclass 1890-1990* (Chicago, Ill.: University of Chicago Press, 1993) 263-65; and U.S. District Court for the District of Connecticut, "Support Court Mission Statement," http://www.ctd.uscourts.gov/support-court .

74. Hirsch, *The Rise of the Penitentiary;* Maconochie, *Crime and Punishment: The Mark System;* Smith, *A Defence of the System of Solitary Confinement.*

oner, and she lives in a limbo of hopes raised and dashed. Experiments with substituting amounts of hard labor for time in the nineteenth century ended badly, because the labor prescribed was harsh, pointless, or insurmountable, and those pushed beyond their capacity for endurance frequently committed suicide.[75]

Possible Responses:

A) Negotiate (as we already do in plea deals) a maximum time measured not by the crime, but by what extent of time we think it would take a reasonable person to complete the service we have jointly decided fits the situation. Then a person convicted of a crime would have the choice between just waiting out the time in confinement, or trying to complete the task early.

B) We could encourage the second path by modeling prisons on the university or on existing "parallel universe" approaches that use grades or work evaluations and promotions, to make the inside operate more like an idealized merit-based job situation outside. Dora Schriro, for example, asked those serving time what kinds of incentives they *wanted* the opportunity to earn, and those in her prisons could earn the opportunity for their families to bring in home-cooked meals to eat with them, or the opportunity for movie nights with popcorn.[76] Those sentenced could also earn points during prison toward better housing afterwards or toward family transportation for visitation, or other benefits for their families, their victims, or their communities. Many prisons already have and already are adopting such a "parallel universe" model; the only difference I propose is that we use this model from the outset of sentencing and not just afterwards.[77] In fact, we

---

75. See John Moore, "Alexander Maconochie's 'Mark System,'" *Prison Service Journal*, 198 (2011): 38–45, for a description of Maconochie's attempts to implement a reformist "parallel universe" labor, not time, system resulting in "misery and disaster": a 15-year old unable to complete his "cranking" task committed suicide, tasks assigned were often "purposeless" because of a lack of available "real" work, and Maconochie resorted to flogging and other corporal punishments..

76. Dora Schriro, "Getting Ready: How Arizona Has Created a 'Parallel Universe' for Inmates," *National Institute of Justice Journal* 263 (2009), https://www.nij.gov/journals/263/pages/getting-ready.aspx

77. These models include California's "Prison Honor Program" (http://www.prisonhonorprogram.org/Fast_Facts.htm); former Arizona and Missouri Commissioner Dora Schriro's "parallel universe" approach to imprisonment (n. 75, above); and

already do this in the context of non-custodial punishments, which use parole-revocation as the "stick," and "services and education" as the carrot. Some have even argued that the federal "supervised release" tail is now wagging the "determinate sentencing" dog, and that we are creating a new *de facto* indeterminate sentencing regime, subject to abuse in part because it is haphazard, unacknowledged, and unexamined.[78]

Objection 2:"Programming"

It is dehumanizing to predict deterministically a person's future by way of statistical models, and it is humiliating and intrusive to live under a totalizing regime of regulations and surveillance. This kind of surveillance does not create a sense of lived meaning, but of mindless and intrusive testing, big-brother nannying, needlessly complex reporting, and bureaucratic make-work and paperwork. Prison programming can be condescending and heteronomous.[79]

Possible Response:

Those of us who have spent time working, teaching, or counseling in prison need to be part of the effort to determine which style, kind, and mode of help to offer in designing helpful "courses of action" for those in prison.[80] Our own work in prison must model the respect for autonomy and dignity that we wish to inculcate. How we speak about what we do matters. Calling people "inmates" or referring to them by numbers or by risk categories is not language that endows

Washington State's prison reforms, examined in Leon Neyfakh, "What Do You Do with the Worst of the Worst?," *Slate*, April 3, 2015 (http://www.slate.com/articles/news_and_politics/crime/2015/04/solitary_confinement_in_washington_state_a_surprising_and_effective_reform.html). See also Jessica Benko, "The Radical Humaneness of Norway's Halden Prison," *New York Times Magazine*, March 26, 2015; accessed at https://www.nytimes.com/2015/03/29/magazine/the-radical-humaneness-of-norways-halden-prison.html. Instead of "static security" of surveillance, the philosophy at Halden is "dynamic security"; as Benko notes, "The guards socialize with inmates every day, in casual conversation, often over tea or coffee or meals."

78. Fiona Dougherty, "Indeterminate Sentencing Returns: The Invention of Supervised Release," *New York University Law Review* 88 (2013), 958.

79. C. S. Lewis, "The Humanitarian Theory of Punishment," *The Twentieth Century: An Australian Quarterly Review*, 3:1 (1949), 5–12; reprinted in Lewis, *God in the Dock*, Walter Hooper, ed. (Grand Rapids, Mich.: William B. Eerdmans, 1970), 287–94.

80. In other words, those who have served time are part of the "us" and the "we."

either the speaker or the spoken-of with responsibility and autonomy. In my view, the more "prison programming" comes to imagine itself on the model of "college teaching and advising and interning," the less dehumanizing it will be. For example, inviting colleges to teach in prison brings the strong norms of the classroom—respect, attention, thoughtfulness, dialogue, etc.—into the prison culture.[81] Those in a classroom, for example, are called "students," not "inmates," "clients," "populations," "cohorts," or "test subjects." We "teach," we do not subject "patients" to "cognitive behavioral conditioning."

Objection 3: Imperialism

What kind of "purpose" are we selling as "atonement?" Are some of us, for example, imposing goal-driven "efficiency and productiveness" values on others of us who see their purpose in life not as "becoming more productive workers," but as building community ties, being good parents, or achieving spiritual growth? Is our model of good citizenship limited to a Protestant work ethic or an American boot-strap narrative—and is that a cultural mismatch? To use Hannah Arendt's terms, are we substituting utility for true action and undermining "meaning" by substituting "goal completion?"[82] Moreover, even if goal-orientation is desirable, is "long-term" goal-oriented thinking really possible in the reentry environments people return to?

A recent article in the *British Journal of Criminology* illustrates the difficulty. The authors tracked youth who were involved in "time-management" programs in prison and who were taught to plan ahead and work incrementally toward longer-term goals. But the world into which they were released didn't operate like that. In chaotic environments, survival requires flexibility, nimbleness in altering course un-

---

81. The under-appreciated norms of the classroom are highlighted and contrasted with a "social science" view of humans in Philippe Nonet, "In the matter of *Green v. Recht*," *California Law Review* 75 (1987), 363..

82. Arendt phrases the tension as follows: "The growing meaninglessness of the modern world is perhaps nowhere more clearly foreshadowed than in this identification of meaning and end. Meaning, which can never be the aim of action and yet, inevitably, will rise out of human deeds after the action itself has come to an end, was now pursued with the same machinery of intentions and of organized means as were the particular and direct aims of concrete action—with the result that it was as though meaning itself had departed from the world." Hannah Arendt, *Between Past and Future: Eight Exercises in Political Thought* (London: Penguin, 2006), 78-79 (originally published in 1961):

der changed circumstances, and being open to taking short-term risks and accepting short-term benefits. Long-term planning and sticking to a disciplined schedule doesn't pay off, because the looked-for goal evaporates before it can be realized.[83]

Possible Response:

We need to recognize that successful lives can be defined in various ways. Again, on the model of college advising, we must tailor prison experience and activity to the individual and community and family situation as much as we can. Vocational training in prison must be connected to realistic opportunities on the outside. Creating a trajectory inside the prison that doesn't work outside is counterproductive. Bridges between prison and jobs and communities are essential and community NGOs should be and are playing a bigger role here. Those who have made it through prison and reentry successfully have key insights that need to be heard by those of us—whether legislators or scholars—who are making or shaping prison policies.[84]

Objection 4: Racism

If we require sentencing as service, given our history and the entrenched institutional and unconscious racism, won't this solution risk reinventing the humiliating and dehumanizing system of prison labor that was historically "slavery by another name?"[85]

Possible Response:

Given our history, this barrier is the most difficult of all. One way to try to avoid racial disparity is to keep minor crimes and drug crimes out of the system and ensure that the service for more serious crimes is skilled and significant and emphasizes the connection with victimized communities. Offenders and victims in our criminal justice system

---

83. Valli Rajah, Ronald Kramer, and Hung-En Sung, "The Mis-Synchronization of Juvenile Reform: Competing Constructions of Temporality and Risk among Rehabilitation Programs and Young Offenders," *British Journal of Criminology*, 55:1 (2015), 184–202.

84. See Just Leadership, https://www.justleadershipusa.org/about-us/; and The Phoenix Association of Connecticut, http://www.phoenixassociation.org/

85. See Douglas A. Blackmon, *Slavery by Another Name* (New York: Random House, 2008), a detailed account of convict-leasing practices post-Civil War, and documenting from court records how black men were routinely charged with minor fine-only offenses around harvest time, which they would have to "work off."

tend to come from the same "million-dollar blocks," neighborhoods where we are paying more than a million dollars per block to police and incarcerate people.[86] So, perhaps those communities should play a larger role in determining what and how offenders should give back. As Jonathan Simon has proposed, "A fund to subsidize the first-year experience of families, or other kin networks, that agree to take in a released prisoner could begin to rebuild the kind of effective exchange that once existed between parole and community."[87] Toxic neighborhoods, however, may not be able to bootstrap themselves into health, and may require inter-community partnerships to attract jobs and legal commerce. Community Reentry Roundtables, which are active in Connecticut, for example, are a great place to start thinking about these questions. In a world of structural racism, moreover, it would be key for minority communities to be making the calls about what and how policing, re-entry, and service sentencing would be implemented.[88]

All of these "how to" questions have good answers in current research. But one cannot expect "programming" to be a panacea, and it does hold dangers that may even be greater than serving "mere time." In the end, atonement is primarily about healing people and relationships, not "institutional programming," "reducing recidivism," and certainly not "social engineering." I've sat through and read through hours of testimony from those who have successfully come back from prison. So many successful reentry stories I've heard begin, "Well, there was this one C.O., and she took time to [get to know me, talk to me, work with

---

86. Todd Clear, *Imprisoning Communities: How Mass Incarceration Makes Disadvantaged Neighborhoods Worse* (New York: Oxford University Press, 2009); Bruce Western, *Punishment and Inequality in America* (New York: Russell Sage Foundation, 2006); and Devah Pager, "The Mark of a Criminal Record," *American Journal of Sociology* 108:5 (2003), 937-975.

87. See Jonathan Simon, *Poor Discipline: Parole and the Social Control of the Underclass 1890–1990* (Chicago, Ill.: University of Chicago Press, 1993), 264.

88. Community should be a fluid idea, not one that reenacts racism and totalitarianism or the "total institution." George Pavlich suggests the idea of Derridean "hospitality" as a better fit, here, and I agree. Again, the classroom model of a community built on norms of respectful listening is a kind of ideal type that I mean to gesture towards. See George Pavlich, "What are the Dangers as Well as the Promises of Community Involvement?" *Critical Issues in Restorative Justice* (Monsey, New York: Criminal Justice Press/Willow Tree Press, 2004) 173-84.

me] and she said [I had this potential and there were other possible futures for me]," or "The victim's father wrote me and told me that I was more than my crime and that I should use my life to give back what I had taken," or "My [mom/son/father] kept coming to visit me week after week and, seeing the sorrow on their face, I knew I had to change." Yet these very human moments of connection, trust, forgiveness, and encouragement are precisely what cannot be refined into a repeatable, transferable, empirically verifiable, successful "program." The question we should be asking is, How might we think about our response to criminal conduct in a way that maximizes the opportunities for these meaningful interactions and relationships to happen?

The answer, again, is not mysterious.[89] From the extensive empirical research and practice done across the world, programs that work to make prison time meaningful usually involve:

1) modeling and practicing trust, patience, and respect in words and actions;

2) creating opportunity for dialogue, creative expression, reflection, speech and feedback among all stakeholders (including corrections officers, victims, formerly incarcerated persons, and community members);

---

89. See above at note 71. To restate: if, in the time that has passed between the commission of a criminal act and an offender's conviction for that act the offender has lived so as to make clear a change of path, the purpose served by incarceration is difficult to discern. For a small sample of literature expressing this view, see Washington Institute of Public Policy, *Criminal Justice* http://www.wsipp.wa.gov/Reports/PolicyArea/ , 2; U.S. Department of Justice, National Institute of Corrections, *Annotated Bibliography, Evidence Based Practices in the Criminal Justice System*, http://static.nicic.gov/Library/026917.pdf; Department of Justice, *Roadmap to Reentry*, https://www.justice.gov/reentry/roadmap-reentry-reducing-recidivism-through-reentry-federal-bureau-prisons; Doran Larson, "Why Scandinavian Prisons are Superior," *The Atlantic*, September 24, 2013 (https://www.theatlantic.com/international/archive/2013/09/why-scandinavian-prisons-are-superior/279949/); Yale Law School, *Detention on a Global Scale: Punishment and Beyond* (New Haven, Conn.: Liman Publications, 2015); Yale Law School, *Isolation and Reintegration: Punishment Circa 2014* (New Haven, Conn.: Liman Publications, 2014); and Austin Sarat, ed., "The Beautiful Prison," *Studies in Law, Politics, and Society* 64 (2014): Special Issue. A number of independent agencies pursue work allied with these ideas, including the Vera Institute of Justice (https://www.vera.org/), The Sentencing Project (http://www.sentencingproject.org/), Penal Reform International (https://www.penalreform.org/), the Council of State Governments Justice Center (https://csgjusticecenter.org/), and the Pew Trusts' Public Safety Performance Project (http://www.pewtrusts.org/en/projects/public-safety-performance-project).

3) tailoring the response of the criminal justice system to the particular stakeholders' needs and concerns and family and community context, including, where appropriate, group therapy and family involvement in mental health and addiction services;

4) allowing as much choice and autonomy in the prison and reentry process as possible in a "parallel universe" approach;

5) maintaining staffing levels, supervising well, and keeping successful staffing consistent over time;

6) providing long-term, stable funding of ideas that work, instead of gutting the easily-severable programming budget every time there is a corrections budget crisis;

7) recruiting committed, visionary people to change the culture of prisons, including victims and those with prison experience;

8) making prisons more transparent and more responsive to partnerships with NGOs;

9) paying, protecting, and training prison staff well, and giving them a sense of community and purpose instead of a sense that they, too, are "doing time" until retirement;

10) enabling the voices of those of us who are or who have been in prison and their families to be heard in political and artistic dialogue and reform projects, so that we understand "prisoners" to be neighbors, siblings, children, and parents, and not monsters and strangers;

11) investing in and supporting the families of the incarcerated that are our primary, and all too often sole, re-entry supports;

12) reevaluating state contracts for and around prisons to avoid the "fixed costs" of poorly functioning institutions that make change impossibly expensive;

13) closing many prisons; substituting cheaper and more effective community-based programming; and

14) making diversion and programming, not prison, the default option. Prison should be a last resort, not the "only social service agency that can't turn you down."[90]

In short, instead of trying to create institutions that are designed to make people do "mere time" (which is neither what is, nor what should

---

90. Joseph Lea, Trinity College, teacher and former prison librarian.

be, happening), we should acknowledge upfront the way the best prisons are actually run, and create sentencing practices that provide support and scope for meaningful action.

◉

Postscript

I can't help but hear the lament of penitentiary-advocate George Washington Smith, when he confronted the actual horrors of solitary confinement and understood how his imagined heaven had created a hell: "the kind accents of mercy were never heard; the mild tones of persuasion, the language of earnest expostulation."[91] Like his vision of prison as a garden of calm, safe communion with God, the ideal I seek requires a form of love that cannot be institutionalized by rule. Perhaps my hoping for a "college in prison" ideal is as foolish as Smith's assumption that solitary confinement as penitence could be institutionalized without the horrors of "the hole." Perhaps "sentencing as service" cannot be other than another round of slavery, another iteration of the violence of Foucauldian discipline. Perhaps it is always the case that what is intended as a reform becomes a new form of oppression. And then the new form of oppression must be reformed again. We are human, living in time from memory to expectation, and therefore we must approach any attempt at atonement (whether individual or institutional) with humility, acknowledging that we will fail and must continue to try and to try again. We will never get it right, but maybe the fact that we keep trying is itself a form of compassion for suffering that helps keep institutions human, and, one hopes, humane.

---

91. Smith, *A Defence of the System of Solitary Confinement*, 36.

Appendix:
Supreme Court decisions of note

Editor's note: On the following pages the author presents excerpts from six Supreme Court Opinions that touch on aspects of the argument presented here:

- *In re: Medley,* 134 U.S. 160 (1890)
- *Ruiz v. Texas,* 580 U.S. _____, 16-7792 (March 7, 2017); Justice Breyer, dissenting from denial of certiorari
- *Ewing v. California,* 538 U.S. 11, 123 S. Ct. 1179 (2003)
- *Brown v. Plata,* 563 U.S. 493, 131 S. Ct. 1910 (2011)
- *Pepper v. United States,* 562 U.S. 476, 131 S. Ct. 1229 (2011)
- *Miller v. Alabama,* 567 U.S. 460 (2012)

The author's selections are meant to provide readers with the key arguments of these opinions touching on the arguments presented in the essay, and not to serve as a complete record of these opinions. We have indicated editorial choices through the use of ellipses [....] following standard typographical practice.

In reprinting these opinions, we have left intact the idiosyncratic way in which Supreme Court opinions do the work of citing their sources. *United States Reports* is the official record of Supreme Court opinions and dissents; because opinions often refer to other, previous opinions, it is typically the case that the final citation of a case is not known for some years after an opinion is handed down.

So, for example, an opinion of the court itself is often cited with a style like "134 U.S. 160"—the citation for *In re: Medley*—which translates to "volume 134 of *United States Reports*, beginning at page 160";

and "*Ewing v. California,* 538 U.S. 11, 123 S. Ct. 1179 (2003)" means that the opinion for *Ewing* can be found in volume 538 of *United States Reports,* as well as in volume 123 of the *Supreme Court Reporter,* the first place in which opinions of the court are published.

From time to time, particularly in the case of more recent opinions, the final editions of *United States Reports* have not yet been compiled. In such cases, a reference that may appear to be blank (as, for example, in the citation for *Ruiz v. Texas* found at the beginning of this note) will indicate to the reader other references through which the material may be found.

In rendering its opinions, the Supreme Court often cites the opinions of lower federal and state courts. These are found in a variety of sources, including the *Federal Reporter,* first, second, and third series (denoted F., F.2d., and F.3d.), containing the records of federal district and appellate court proceedings; the decisions of state appellate courts, gathered in a series of volumes gathering opinions in geographic areas, for example the *North Eastern Reporter,* first and second series (N.E. and N.E. 2d); and so on.

Occasionally the opinions will also refer to articles from scholarly law journals, the titles of which are nearly always abbreviated; for the convenience of non-specialists we have indicated the full names of these journals.

Careful readers will also note that the ways in which a Supreme Court opinion cites materials other than court opinions (books, scholarly articles, statute laws, etc.) varies somewhat from the usual style of footnotes in scholarly books; we have left the Court's style intact here.

SUPREME COURT OF THE UNITED STATES

MEDLEY, PETITIONER
(134 U.S. 160)
Argued: January 15, 1890.
Decided: March 3, 1890.

MR. JUSTICE MILLER delivered the opinion of the Court.

This is an application to this court by James J Medley for a writ of habeas corpus, the object of which is to relieve him from the imprisonment in which he is held by J A. Lamping; warden of the state penitentiary of the State of Colorado.

The petitioner is held a prisoner under sentence of death pronounced by the District Court of the Second District of the State of Colorado for the county of Arapahoe....

The petitioner enumerates some twenty variances between the statute in force at the time the crime was committed and that under which he was sentenced to punishment in the present case, all of which are claimed to be changes to his prejudice and injury, and therefore *ex post facto* within the meaning of section 10, article 1 of the Constitution of the United States, which declares that no State shall pass any bill of attainder or *ex post facto law.*

The first of these [variances], and perhaps the most important, is that which declares that the warden shall keep such convict in solitary confinement until the infliction of the death penalty. The former law, the act of 1883, contained no such provision. It declared that every person convicted of murder in the first degree should suffer death, and every person convicted of murder of the second degree should suffer imprisonment in the penitentiary for a term of not less than ten years, which might extend to life, and it declared that the manner of inflicting the punishment of death should be by hanging the person convicted by the neck until death, at such time as the court should direct, not less than fifteen nor more than twenty-five days from the time sentence was pronounced, unless for good cause the court or governor might prolong the time. The prisoner was to be kept in the county jail under the control of the sheriff of the county, who was the officer charged with the execution of the sentence of the court. Solitary confinement was neither authorized by the former statute, nor was its practice in use in regard to prisoners awaiting the punishment of death.

This matter of solitary confinement is not, as seems to be supposed by counsel, and as is suggested in an able opinion on this statute, furnished us by the brief of the counsel for the State, by Judge Hayt, (in the case of Henry Tyson,) a mere unimportant regulation as to the safe-keeping of the prisoner, and is not relieved of its objectionable features by the qualifying language, that no person shall be allowed access to said convict except his attendants, counsel, physician, a spiritual adviser of his own selection, and members of his family, and then only in accordance with prison regulations.

Solitary confinement as a punishment for crime has a very interesting history of its own, in almost all countries where imprisonment is one of the means of punishment. In a very exhaustive article on this subject in the American Cyclopædia, Volume XIII, under the word "Prison" this history is given. In that article it is said that the first plan adopted when public attention was called to the evils of congregating persons in masses without employment, was the solitary prison connected with the Hospital San Michele at Rome, in 1703, but little known prior to the experiment in Walnut Street Penitentiary in Philadelphia in 1787. The peculiarities of this system were the complete isolation of the prisoner from all human society and his confinement in a cell of considerable size, so arranged that he had no direct intercourse with or sight of any human being, and no employment or instruction. Other prisons on the same plan, which were less liberal in the size of their cells and the perfection of their appliances, were erected in Massachusetts, New Jersey, Maryland and some of the other States. But experience demonstrated that there were serious objections to it. A considerable number of the prisoners fell, after even a short confinement, into a semi-fatuous condition, from which it was next to impossible to arouse them, and others became violently insane, others, still, committed suicide, while those who stood the ordeal better were not generally reformed, and in most cases did not recover sufficient mental activity to be of any subsequent service to the community. It became evident that some changes must be made in the system, and the *separate* system was originated by the Philadelphia Society for Ameliorating the Miseries of Public Prisons, founded in 1787....

Instead of confinement in the ordinary county prison of the place where he and his friends reside, where they may, under the control of the sheriff, see him and visit him, where the sheriff and his attendants must see him, where his religious adviser and his legal counsel may often visit him without any hindrance of law on the subject, the convict is transferred to a place where imprisonment always implies disgrace, and which, as this court has judicially decided in *Ex parte Wilson*, 114 U. S. 417, *Mackin v United States*, 117 U.S. 348, *Parkinson v United States*, 121 U. S. 281, and *United States v De Walt*, 128 U. S. 393, is itself an infamous punishment, and is there to be kept in "solitary confinement," the primary meaning of which phrase we have already explained....

Even the statutory amelioration is a very limited one. By the words "his attendants" in the statute, is evidently meant the officers of the prison and subordinates, who must necessarily furnish him with his food and his clothing, and make inspection every day that he still exists. They may be forbidden by prison regulations, however, from holding any conversation with him. The attendance of the counsel can only be casual, and a very few interviews, one or two, perhaps, are all that he would have before his death, and that of the physician not at all, unless he was so sick as to require it, and the spiritual adviser of his own selection, and the members of his family, are all dependent for their opportunities of seeing the prisoner upon the regulations of the prison. The solitary confinement, then, which is meant by the statute, remains of the essential character of that mode of prison life as it originally was prescribed and carried out, to mark them as examples of the just punishment of the worst crimes of the human race.

It seems to us that the considerations which we have here suggested show that the solitary confinement to which the prisoner was subjected by the statute of Colorado of 1889, and by the judgment of the court in pursuance of that statute, was an additional punishment of the most important and painful character, and is, therefore, forbidden by this provision of the Constitution of the United States.

Another provision of the statute, which is supposed to be liable to this objection, of its *ex post facto* character, is found in section 3, in which the particular day and hour of the execution of the sentence within the week specified by the warrant shall be fixed by the warden, and he shall invite to be present certain persons named, to wit, a chaplain, a physician, a surgeon, the spiritual adviser of the convict, and six reputable citizens of the State of full age, and that the time fixed by said warden for such execution shall be by him kept secret, and in no manner divulged except privately to said persons invited by him to be present as aforesaid, and such persons shall not divulge such invitation to any person or persons whomsoever, nor in any manner disclose the time of such execution. And section six provides that any person who shall violate or omit to comply with the requirements of section three of the act shall be punished by fine or imprisonment. We understand the meaning of this section to be that within the one week mentioned in the judgment of the court the warden is charged with the power of fixing the precise day and hour when the prisoner shall be executed, that he is forbidden to communicate that time to the prisoner; that all persons whom he is directed to invite to be present at the execution are forbidden to communicate that time to him, and that, in fact, the prisoner is to be kept in utter ignorance of the day and hour when his mortal life shall be terminated by hanging, until the moment arrives when this act is to be done.

Objections are made to this provision as being a departure from the law as it stood before, and as being an additional punishment to the prisoner, and therefore *ex post facto.*

It is obvious that it confers upon the warden of the penitentiary a power which had heretofore been solely confided to the court, and is therefore a departure from the law as it stood when the crime was committed.

Nor can we withhold our conviction of the proposition that when a prisoner sentenced by a court to death is confined in the penitentiary awaiting the execution of the sentence, one of the most horrible feelings to which he can be subjected during that time is the uncertainty during the whole of it, which may exist for the period of four weeks, as to the precise time when his execution shall take place. Notwithstanding the argument that under all former systems of administering capital punishment the officer appointed to execute it had a right to select the time of *the day* when it should be done, this new power of fixing any day and hour during a period of a week for the execution is a new and important power conferred on that officer, and is a departure from the law as it existed at the time the offence was committed, and with its secrecy must be accompanied by an immense mental anxiety amounting to a great increase of the offender's punishment.

There are other provisions of the statute pointed out in the argument of counsel, which are alleged to be subject to the same objection, but we think the two we have mentioned are quite sufficient to show that the Constitution of the United States is violated by this statute as applied to crimes committed before it came into force....

SUPREME COURT OF THE UNITED STATES

No. 16A841 (16–7792)

ROLANDO RUIZ v. TEXAS

ON APPLICATION FOR STAY

[March 7, 2017]

The application for stay of execution of sentence of death presented to **Justice Thomas** and by him referred to the Court is denied.

Justice Breyer, dissenting.

Petitioner Rolando Ruiz has been on death row for 22 years, most
of which he has spent in permanent solitary confinement. Mr. Ruiz
argues that his execution "violates the Eighth Amendment" because
it "follow[s] lengthy [death row] incarceration in traumatic conditions," principally his "permanent solitary confinement." Petition 25. I
believe his claim is a strong one, and we should consider it.

This Court long ago, speaking of a period of only four weeks of
imprisonment prior to execution, said that a prisoner's uncertainty
before execution is "one of the most horrible feelings to which he can
be subjected." *In re Medley*, 134 U. S. 160, 172 (1890). Here the prisoner
has undergone death row imprisonment, not of four weeks, but of 22
years.

Moreover, in 1890, this Court recognized long-standing "serious
objections" to extended solitary confinement. The Court pointed to
studies showing that "[a] considerable number of the prisoners fell,
after even a short confinement, into a semi-fatuous condition, from

which it was next to impossible to arouse them, and others became violently insane; others still, committed suicide; while those who stood the ordeal better were not generally reformed, and in most cases did not recover sufficient mental activity to be of any subsequent service to the community. It became evident that some changes must be made in the system," as "its main feature of solitary confinement was found to be too severe." *Id.*, at 168.

Others have more recently pointed out that a terrible "human toll" is "wrought by extended terms of isolation" and that "[y]ears on end of near-total isolation exact a terrible" psychiatric "price." *Davis v. Ayala,* 576 U. S. ___, __ – __ [135 S. Ct. 2187, 2208–2210] (2015) (KENNEDY, J., concurring) (quoting *In re Medley,* supra, at 170). As a result it has been suggested that, "[i]n a case that present[s] the issue," this Court should determine whether extended solitary confinement survives Eighth Amendment scrutiny. *Davis v. Ayala,* supra, at 3–4 (opinion of KENNEDY, J.). This I believe is an appropriate case to conduct that constitutional scrutiny.

Here the "human toll" that accompanies extended solitary confinement is exacerbated by the fact that execution is in the offing. Moreover, Mr. Ruiz has developed symptoms long associated with solitary confinement, namely severe anxiety and depression, suicidal thoughts, hallucinations, disorientation, memory loss, and sleep difficulty. Further, the lower courts have recognized that Mr. Ruiz has been diligent in pursuing his claims, finding the 22–year delay attributable to the State or the lower courts. *Ruiz v. Quarterman,* 504 F. 3d 523, 530 (CA5 2007) (quoting *Ruiz v. Dretke,* 2005 WL 2620193, *2 (WD Tex., Oct. 13, 2005)). Nor are Mr. Ruiz's 20 years of solitary confinement attributable to any special penological problem or need. They arise simply from the fact that he is a prisoner awaiting execution. App[endix]. E to Petition 16.

If extended solitary confinement alone raises serious constitutional questions, then 20 years of solitary confinement, all the while under threat of execution, must raise similar questions, and to a rare degree, and with particular intensity. That is why I would grant a stay of execution, allowing the Court to examine the record more fully.

SUPREME COURT OF THE UNITED STATES

EWING v. CALIFORNIA
(538 U.S. 11)

Argued: November 5, 2002.
Decided: March 5, 2003.

JUSTICE O'CONNOR announced the judgment of the Court and delivered an opinion, in which **THE CHIEF JUSTICE** and **JUSTICE KENNEDY** join.

In this case, we decide whether the Eighth Amendment prohibits the State of California from sentencing a repeat felon to a prison term of 25 years to life under the State's "Three Strikes and You're Out" law.

I
A

California's three strikes law reflects a shift in the State's sentencing policies toward incapacitating and deterring repeat offenders who threaten the public safety. The law was designed "to ensure longer prison sentences and greater punishment for those who commit a felony and have been previously convicted of serious and/or violent felony offenses." Cal. Penal Code Ann. § 667(b) (West 1999). On March 3, 1993, California Assemblymen Bill Jones and Jim Costa introduced Assembly Bill 971, the legislative version of what would later become the three strikes law. The Assembly Committee on Public Safety defeated the bill only weeks later. Public outrage over the defeat sparked a voter initiative to add Proposition 184, based loosely on the bill, to the ballot in the November 1994 general election.

On October 1, 1993, while Proposition 184 was circulating, 12-year-old Polly Klaas was kidnap[p]ed from her home in Petaluma, California. Her admitted killer, Richard Allen Davis, had a long criminal history that included two prior kidnaping convictions. Davis had served only half of his most recent sentence (16 years for kidnapping, assault, and burglary). Had Davis served his entire sentence, he would still have been in prison on the day that Polly Klaas was kidnap[p]ed.

Polly Klaas' murder galvanized support for the three strikes initiative. Within days, Proposition 184 was on its way to becoming the fastest qualifying initiative in California history. On January 3, 1994, the sponsors of Assembly Bill 971 resubmitted an amended version of the bill that conformed to Proposition 184. On January 31, 1994, Assembly Bill 971 passed the Assembly by a 63 to 9 margin. The Senate passed it by a 29 to 7 margin on March 3, 1994. Governor Pete Wilson signed the bill into law on March 7, 1994. California voters approved Proposition 184 by a margin of 72 to 28 percent on November 8, 1994.

California thus became the second State to enact a three strikes law. In November 1993, the voters of Washington State approved their own three strikes law, Initiative 593, by a margin of 3 to 1. U. S. Dept. of Justice, National Institute of Justice, J. Clark, J. Austin, & D. Henry, "Three Strikes and You're Out": A Review of State Legislation 1 (Sept. 1997) (hereinafter Review of State Legislation). Between 1993 and 1995, 24 States and the Federal Government enacted three strikes laws. *Ibid.* Though the three strikes laws vary from State to State, they share a common goal of protecting the public safety by providing lengthy prison terms for habitual felons.

B

California's current three strikes law consists of two virtually identical statutory schemes "designed to increase the prison terms of repeat felons." *People v. Superior Court of San Diego Cty. ex rel. Romero*, 13 Cal. 4th 497, 504, 917 P. 2d 628, 630 (1996) (*Romero*). When a defendant is convicted of a felony, and he has previously been convicted of one or more prior felonies defined as "serious" or "violent" in Cal. Penal Code Ann. §§ 667.5 and 1192.7 (West Supp. 2002), sentencing is conducted pursuant to the three strikes law. Prior convictions must be alleged in the charging document, and the defendant has a right to a jury determination that the prosecution has proved the prior convictions beyond a reasonable doubt. § 1025; § 1158 (West 1985).

If the defendant has one prior "serious" or "violent" felony conviction, he must be sentenced to "twice the term otherwise provided as punishment for the current felony conviction." § 667(e)(1) (West 1999); § 1170.12(c)(1) (West Supp. 2002). If the defendant has two or more prior "serious" or "violent" felony convictions, he must receive "an indeterminate term of life imprisonment." § 667(e)(2)(A) (West 1999); § 1170.12(c)(2)(A) (West Supp. 2002). Defendants sentenced to life under the three strikes law become eligible for parole on a date calculated by reference to a "minimum term," which is the greater of (a) three times the term otherwise provided for the current conviction, (b) 25 years, or (c) the term determined by the court pursuant to § 1170 for the underlying conviction, including any enhancements. §§ 667(e)(2)(A)(i)–(iii) (West 1999); §§ 1170.12(c)(2)(A)(i)–(iii) (West Supp. 2002)....

C

On parole from a 9-year prison term, petitioner Gary Ewing walked into the pro shop of the El Segundo Golf Course in Los Angeles County on March 12, 2000. He walked out with three golf clubs, priced at $399 apiece, concealed in his pants leg. A shop employee, whose suspicions were aroused when he observed Ewing limp out of the pro shop, telephoned the police. The police apprehended Ewing in the parking lot.

Ewing is no stranger to the criminal justice system. In 1984, at the age of 22, he pleaded guilty to theft. The court sentenced him to six months in jail (suspended), three years' probation, and a $300 fine. In 1988, he was convicted of felony grand theft auto and sentenced to one year in jail and three years' probation. After Ewing completed probation, however, the sentencing court reduced the crime to a misdemeanor, permitted Ewing to withdraw his guilty plea, and dismissed the case. In 1990, he was convicted of petty theft with a prior and sentenced to 60 days in the county jail and three years' probation. In 1992, Ewing was convicted of battery and sentenced to 30 days in the county jail and two years' summary probation. One month later, he was convicted of theft and sentenced to 10 days in the county jail and 12 months' probation. In January 1993, Ewing was convicted of burglary and sentenced to 60 days in the county jail and one year's summary probation. In February 1993, he was convicted of possessing drug paraphernalia and sentenced to six months in the county jail and three years' probation. In July 1993, he was convicted of appropriating lost property and sentenced to 10 days in the county jail and two years' summary probation. In September 1993, he was convicted of unlawfully possessing a firearm and trespassing and sentenced to 30 days in the county jail and one year's probation.

In October and November 1993, Ewing committed three burglaries and one robbery at a Long Beach, California, apartment complex over a 5-week period. He awakened one of his victims, asleep on her living room sofa, as he tried to disconnect her video cassette recorder from the television in that room. When she screamed, Ewing ran out the front door. On another occasion, Ewing accosted a victim in the mailroom of the apartment complex. Ewing claimed to have a gun and ordered the victim to hand over his wallet. When the victim resisted, Ewing produced a knife and forced the victim back to the apartment itself. While Ewing rifled through the bedroom, the victim fled the apartment screaming for help. Ewing absconded with the victim's money and credit cards.

On December 9, 1993, Ewing was arrested on the premises of the apartment complex for trespassing and lying to a police officer. The knife used in the robbery and a glass cocaine pipe were later found in the back seat of the patrol car used to transport Ewing to the police station. A jury convicted Ewing of first-degree robbery and three counts of residential burglary. Sentenced to nine years and eight months in prison, Ewing was paroled in 1999.

Only 10 months later, Ewing stole the golf clubs at issue in this case. He was charged with, and ultimately convicted of, one count of felony grand theft of personal property in excess of $400. See Cal. Penal Code Ann. § 484 (West Supp. 2002); § 489 (West 1999). As required by the three strikes law, the prosecutor formally alleged, and the trial court later found, that Ewing had been convicted previously of four serious or violent felonies for the three burglaries and the robbery in the Long Beach apartment complex. See § 667(g) (West 1999); § 1170.12(e) (West Supp. 2002)....

II

C

The Eighth Amendment, which forbids cruel and unusual punishments, contains a "narrow proportionality principle" that "applies to noncapital sentences." *Harmelin v. Michigan,* 501 U. S. 957, 996–997 (1991) (Kennedy, J., concurring in part and concurring in judgment); cf. *Weems v. United States,* 217 U. S. 349, 371 (1910); *Robinson v. California,* 370 U. S. 660, 667 (1962) (applying the Eighth Amendment to the States via the Fourteenth Amendment). We have most recently addressed the proportionality principle as applied to terms of years in a series of cases beginning with *Rummel v. Estelle, supra.*

In *Rummel,* we held that it did not violate the Eighth Amendment for a State to sentence a three-time offender to life in prison with the possibility of parole. *Id.,* at 284–285. Like Ewing, Rummel was sentenced to a lengthy prison term under a recidivism statute. Rummel's two prior offenses were a 1964 felony for "fraudulent use of a credit card to obtain $80 worth of goods or services," and a 1969 felony conviction for "passing a forged check in the amount of $28.36." *Id.,* at 265. His triggering offense was a conviction for felony theft—"obtaining $120.75 by false pretenses." *Id.,* at 266.

This Court ruled that "[h]aving twice imprisoned him for felonies, Texas was entitled to place upon Rummel the onus of one who is simply unable to bring his conduct within the social norms prescribed by the criminal law of the State." *Id.,* at 284. The recidivism statute "is nothing more than a societal decision that when such a person commits yet another felony, he should be subjected to the admittedly serious penalty of incarceration for life, subject only to the State's judgment as to whether to grant him parole." *Id.,* at 278. We noted that this Court "has on occasion stated that the Eighth Amendment prohibits imposition of a sentence that is grossly disproportionate to the severity of the crime." *Id.*, at 271. But "[o]utside the context of capital punishment, successful challenges to the proportionality of particular sentences have been exceedingly rare." *Id.*, at 272. Although we stated that the proportionality principle "would...come into play in the extreme example...if a legislature made overtime parking a felony punishable by life imprisonment," *id.*, at 274, n. 11, we held that "the mandatory life sentence imposed upon this petitioner does not constitute cruel and unusual punishment under the Eighth and Fourteenth Amendments," *id.*, at 285.

In *Hutto v. Davis*, 454 U. S. 370 (1982) (*per curiam*), the defendant was sentenced to two consecutive terms of 20 years in prison for possession with intent to distribute nine ounces of marijuana and distribution of marijuana. We held that such a sentence was constitutional: "In short, *Rummel* stands for the proposition that federal courts should be reluctant to review legislatively mandated terms of imprisonment, and that successful challenges to the proportionality of particular sentences should be exceedingly rare." *Id.*, at 374 (citations and internal quotation marks omitted).

Three years after *Rummel*, in *Solem v. Helm*, 463 U. S. 277, 279 (1983), we held that the Eighth Amendment prohibited "a life sentence without possibility of parole for a seventh nonviolent felony." The triggering offense in *Solem* was "uttering a 'no account' check for $100." *Id.*, at 281. We specifically stated that the Eighth Amendment's ban on cruel and unusual punishments "prohibits...sentences that are disproportionate to the crime committed," and that the "constitutional principle of proportionality has been recognized explicitly in this Court for almost a century." *Id.*, at 284, 286. The *Solem* Court then explained that three factors may be relevant to a determination of whether a sentence is so disproportionate that it violates the Eighth Amendment: "(i) the gravity of the offense and the harshness of the penalty; (ii) the sentences imposed on other criminals in the same jurisdiction; and (iii) the sentences imposed for commission of the same crime in other jurisdictions." *Id.*, at 292.

Applying these factors in *Solem*, we struck down the defendant's sentence of life without parole. We specifically noted the contrast between that sentence and the sentence in *Rummel*, pursuant to which the defendant was eligible for parole. 463 U. S., at 297; see also *id.*, at 300 ("[T]he South Dakota commutation system is fundamentally different from the parole system that was before us in *Rummel*"). Indeed, we explicitly declined to overrule *Rummel*: "[O]ur conclusion today is not inconsistent with *Rummel v. Estelle.*" 463 U. S., at 303, n. 32; see also *id.*, at 288, n. 13 ("[O]ur decision is entirely consistent with this Court's prior cases—including *Rummel v. Estelle*").

Eight years after *Solem*, we grappled with the proportionality issue again in *Harmelin*. *Harmelin* was not a recidivism case, but rather involved a first-time offender convicted of possessing 672 grams of cocaine. He was sentenced to life in prison without possibility of parole. A majority of the Court rejected Harmelin's claim that his sentence was so grossly disproportionate that it violated the Eighth Amendment. The Court, however, could not agree on why his proportionality argument failed. Justice Scalia, joined by The Chief Justice, wrote that the proportionality principle was "an aspect of our death penalty jurisprudence, rather than a generalizable aspect of Eighth Amendment law." 501 U. S. at 994. He would thus have declined to apply gross disproportionality principles except in reviewing capital sentences. *Ibid.*

Justice Kennedy, joined by two other Members of the Court, concurred in part and concurred in the judgment. Justice Kennedy specifically recognized that "[t]he Eighth Amendment proportionality principle also applies to noncapital sentences." *Id.*, at 997. He then identified four principles of proportionality review—"the primacy of the legislature, the variety of legitimate penological schemes, the nature of our federal system, and the requirement that proportionality review be guided by objective factors"—that "inform the final one: The Eighth Amendment does not require strict proportionality between crime and sentence. Rather, it forbids only extreme sentences that are 'grossly disproportionate' to the crime." *Id.*, at 1001 (citing *Solem*, supra, at 288). Justice Kennedy's concurrence also stated that *Solem* "did not mandate" comparative analysis "within and between jurisdictions." 501 U. S., at 1004–1005.

The proportionality principles in our cases distilled in Justice Kennedy's concurrence guide our application of the Eighth Amendment in the new context that we are called upon to consider.

B

For many years, most States have had laws providing for enhanced sentencing of repeat offenders. See, *e. g.*, U. S. Dept. of Justice, Bureau of Justice Assistance, National Assessment of Structured Sentencing (1996). Yet between 1993 and 1995, three strikes laws effected a sea change in criminal sentencing throughout the Nation.[1] These laws responded to widespread public concerns about crime by targeting the class of offenders who pose the greatest threat to public safety: career criminals. As one of the chief architects of California's three strikes law has explained: "Three Strikes was intended to go beyond simply making sentences tougher. It was intended to be a focused effort to create a sentencing policy that would use the judicial system to reduce serious and violent crime." Ardaiz, California's Three Strikes Law: History, Expectations, Consequences, 32 McGeorge L[aw]. Rev[iew]. 1, 12 (2000) (hereinafter Ardaiz).

Throughout the States, legislatures enacting three strikes laws made a deliberate policy choice that individuals who have repeatedly engaged in serious or violent criminal behavior, and whose conduct has not been deterred by more conventional approaches to punishment, must be isolated from society in order to protect the public safety. Though three strikes laws may be relatively new, our tradition of deferring to state legislatures in making and implementing such important policy decisions is longstanding. *Weems*, 217 U. S., at 379; *Gore v. United States*, 357 U. S. 386, 393 [25] (1958); *Payne v. Tennessee*, 501 U. S. 808, 824 (1991); *Rummel*, 445 U. S., at 274; *Solem*, 463 U. S., at

---

1. It is hardly surprising that the statistics relied upon by Justice Breyer show that prior to the enactment of the three strikes law, "*no* one like Ewing could have served more than *10* years in prison." *Post*, at 43 (dissenting opinion) (emphasis added). Profound disappointment with the perceived lenity of criminal sentencing (especially for repeat felons) led to passage of three strikes laws in the first place. See, e. g., Review of State Legislation 1.

290; *Harmelin*, 501 U. S., at 998 (Kennedy, J., concurring in part and concurring in judgment).

Our traditional deference to legislative policy choices finds a corollary in the principle that the Constitution "does not mandate adoption of any one penological theory." *Id.*, at 999 (Kennedy, J., concurring in part and concurring in judgment). A sentence can have a variety of justifications, such as incapacitation, deterrence, retribution, or rehabilitation. See 1 W. LaFave & A. Scott, Substantive Criminal Law § 1.5, pp. 30–36 (1986) (explaining theories of punishment). Some or all of these justifications may play a role in a State's sentencing scheme. Selecting the sentencing rationales is generally a policy choice to be made by state legislatures, not federal courts.

When the California Legislature enacted the three strikes law, it made a judgment that protecting the public safety requires incapacitating criminals who have already been convicted of at least one serious or violent crime. Nothing in the Eighth Amendment prohibits California from making that choice. To the contrary, our cases establish that "States have a valid interest in deterring and segregating habitual criminals." *Parke v. Raley*, 506 U. S. 20, 27 (1992); *Oyler v. Boles*, 368 U. S. 448, 451 (1962) ("[T]he constitutionality of the practice of inflicting severer criminal penalties upon habitual offenders is no longer open to serious challenge"). Recidivism has long been recognized as a legitimate basis for increased punishment. See *Almendarez–Torres v. United States*, 523 U. S. 224, 230 (1998) (recidivism "is as typical a sentencing factor as one might imagine"); *Witte v. United States*, 515 U. S. 389, 400 (1995) ("In repeatedly upholding such recidivism statutes, we have rejected double jeopardy challenges because the enhanced punishment imposed for the later offense...[is] 'a stiffened penalty for the latest crime, which is considered to be an aggravated [26] offense because a repetitive one'" (quoting *Gryger v. Burke*, 334 U. S. 728, 732 (1948))).

California's justification is no pretext. Recidivism is a serious public safety concern in California and throughout the Nation. According to a recent report, approximately 67 percent of former inmates released from state prisons were charged with at least one "serious" new crime within three years of their release. See U. S. Dept. of Justice, Bureau of Justice Statistics, P. Langan & D. Levin, Special Report: Recidivism of Prisoners Released in 1994, p. 1 (June 2002). In particular, released property offenders like Ewing had higher recidivism rates than those released after committing violent, drug, or public-order offenses. *Id.*, at 8. Approximately 73 percent of the property offenders released in 1994 were arrested again within three years, compared to approximately 61 percent of the violent offenders, 62 percent of the public-order offenders, and 66 percent of the drug offenders. *Ibid.*...

To be sure, California's three strikes law has sparked controversy. Critics have doubted the law's wisdom, cost-efficiency, and effectiveness in reaching its goals. See, e. g., Zimring, Hawkins, & Kamin, Punishment and Democracy: Three Strikes and You're Out in California (2001); Vitiello, Three Strikes: Can We Return to Rationality? 87 J[ournal of]. Crim[inal]. [28] L[aw]. & C[riminlogy]. 395, 423 (1997). This criticism is appropriately directed at the legislature, which has primary responsibility for making the difficult policy choices that underlie any criminal sentencing scheme. We do not sit as a "superlegislature" to second-guess these policy choices. It is enough that the State of California has a reasonable basis for believing that dramatically enhanced sentences for habitual felons "advance[s] the goals of [its] criminal justice system in any substantial way." See *Solem*, 463 U. S., at 297, n. 22.

III

Against this backdrop, we consider Ewing's claim that his three strikes sentence of 25 years to life is unconstitutionally disproportionate to his offense of "shoplifting three golf clubs." Brief for Petitioner 6. We first address the gravity of the offense compared to the harshness of the penalty. At the threshold, we note that Ewing incorrectly frames the issue. The gravity of his offense was not merely "shoplifting three golf clubs." Rather, Ewing was convicted of felony grand theft for stealing nearly $1,200 worth of merchandise after previously having been convicted of at least two "violent" or "serious" felonies. Even standing alone, Ewing's theft should not be taken lightly. His crime was certainly not "one of the most passive felonies a person could commit." *Solem*, supra, at 296 (internal quotation marks omitted). To the contrary, the Supreme Court of California has noted the "seriousness" of grand theft in the context of proportionality review. See *In re Lynch*, 8 Cal. 3d 410, 432, n. 20, 503 P. 2d 921, 936, n. 20 (1972). Theft of $1,200 in property is a felony under federal law, 18 U.S.C. § 641, and in the vast majority of States. See App. B to Brief for Petitioner 21a....

In weighing the gravity of Ewing's offense, we must place on the scales not only his current felony, but also his long history of felony recidivism. Any other approach would fail to accord proper deference to the policy judgments that find expression in the legislature's choice of sanctions. In imposing a three strikes sentence, the State's interest is not merely punishing the offense of conviction, or the "triggering" offense: "[I]t is in addition the interest...in dealing in a harsher manner with those who by repeated criminal acts have shown that they are simply incapable of conforming to the norms of society as established by its criminal law." *Rummel*, 445 U. S., at 276; *Solem*, supra, at 296. To give full effect to the State's choice of this legitimate penological goal, our proportionality review of Ewing's sentence must take that goal into account.

Ewing's sentence is justified by the State's public-safety interest in incapacitating and deterring recidivist felons, and amply supported by his own long, serious criminal record.[2] Ewing has been convicted of numerous misdemeanor and felony offenses, served nine separate terms of incarceration, and committed most of his crimes while on probation or parole. His prior "strikes" were serious felonies including

2. Justice Breyer argues that including Ewing's grand theft as a triggering offense cannot be justified on "property-crime-related incapacitation grounds" because such crimes do not count as prior strikes. *Post*, at 51. But the State's interest in dealing with repeat felons like Ewing is not so limited. As we have explained, the overarching objective of the three strikes law is to prevent serious or violent offenders like Ewing from repeating their criminal behavior. See Cal. Penal Code Ann. § 667(b) (West 1999) ("It is the intent of the Legislature...to ensure longer prison sentences and greater punishment for those who commit a felony and have been previously convicted of serious and/or violent felony offenses"). The California Legislature therefore made a "deliberate policy decision...that the gravity of the new felony should not be a determinative factor in 'triggering' the application of the Three Strikes Law." Ardaiz 9. Neither the Eighth Amendment nor this Court's precedent forecloses that legislative choice.

robbery and three residential burglaries. To be sure, Ewing's sentence is a long one. But it reflects a rational legislative judgment, entitled to deference, that offenders who have committed serious or violent felonies and who continue to commit felonies must be incapacitated. The State of California "was entitled to place upon [Ewing] the onus of one who is simply unable to bring his conduct within the social norms prescribed by the criminal law of the State." *Rummel*, supra, at 284. Ewing's is not "the rare case in which a threshold comparison of the crime committed and the sentence imposed leads to an inference of gross disproportionality." *Harmelin*, 501 U. S., at 1005 (Kennedy, J., concurring in part and concurring in judgment).

We hold that Ewing's sentence of 25 years to life in prison, imposed for the offense of felony grand theft under the three strikes law, is not grossly disproportionate and therefore does not violate the Eighth Amendment's prohibition on cruel and unusual punishments. The judgment of the California Court of Appeal is affirmed.

It is so ordered.

[Concurring and dissenting opinions omitted.]

SUPREME COURT OF THE UNITED STATES

BROWN, GOVERNOR OF CALIFORNIA, ET AL., V.
PLATA, ET AL.
(563 U.S. 493)

Argued: November 30, 2010.
Decided: May 23, 2011.

JUSTICE KENNEDY delivered the opinion of the Court.

This case arises from serious constitutional violations in California's prison system. The violations have persisted for years. They remain uncorrected....

The appeal presents the question whether the remedial order issued by the three-judge court is consistent with requirements and procedures set forth in a congressional statute, the Prison Litigation Reform Act of 1995 (PLRA). 18 U.S.C. §3626; see Appendix A, infra . The order leaves the choice of means to reduce overcrowding to the discretion of state officials. But absent compliance through new construction, out-of-state transfers, or other means—or modification of the order upon a further showing by the State—the State will be required to release some number of prisoners before their full sentences have been served. High recidivism rates must serve as a warning that mistaken or premature release of even one prisoner can cause injury and harm. The release of prisoners in large numbers—assuming the State finds no other way to comply with the order—is a matter of undoubted, grave concern.

At the time of trial, California's correctional facilities held some 156,000 persons. This is nearly double the number that California's prisons were designed to hold, and California has been ordered to reduce its prison population to 137.5% of design capacity. By the three-judge court's own estimate, the required population reduction could be as high as 46,000 persons. Although the State has reduced the population by at least 9,000 persons during the pendency of this appeal, this means a further reduction of 37,000 persons could be required. As will be noted, the reduction need not be accomplished in an indiscriminate manner or in these substantial numbers if satisfactory, alternate remedies or means for compliance are devised. The State may employ measures, including good-time credits and diversion of low-risk offenders and technical parole violators to community-based programs, that will mitigate the order's impact. The population reduction potentially required is nevertheless of unprecedented sweep and extent.

Yet so too is the continuing injury and harm resulting from these serious constitutional violations. For years the medical and mental health care provided by California's prisons has fallen short of minimum constitutional requirements and has failed to meet prisoners' basic health needs. Needless suffering and death have been the well-documented result. Over the whole course of years during which this litigation has been pending, no other remedies have been found to be sufficient. Efforts to remedy the violation have been frustrated by severe overcrowding in California's prison system. Short term gains in the provision of care have been eroded by the long-term effects of severe and pervasive overcrowding.

Overcrowding has overtaken the limited resources of prison staff; imposed demands well beyond the capacity of medical and mental health facilities; and created unsanitary and unsafe conditions that make progress in the provision of care difficult or impossible to achieve. The overcrowding is the "primary cause of the violation of a Federal right," 18 U.S.C. §3626(a)(3)(E)(i), specifically the severe and unlawful mistreatment of prisoners through grossly inadequate provision of medical and mental health care.

This Court now holds that the PLRA does authorize the relief afforded in this case and that the court-mandated population limit is necessary to remedy the violation of prisoners' constitutional rights. The order of the three-judge court, subject to the right of the State to seek its modification in appropriate circumstances, must be affirmed.

I

A

The degree of overcrowding in California's prisons is exceptional. California's prisons are designed to house a population just under 80,000, but at the time of the three-judge court's decision the population was almost double that. The State's prisons had operated at around 200% of design capacity for at least 11 years. Prisoners are crammed into spaces neither designed nor intended to house inmates. As many as 200 prisoners may live in a gymnasium, monitored by as few as two or three correctional officers. App. 1337–1338, 1350; see Appendix B, *infra*. As many as 54 prisoners may share a single toilet. App. 1337.

The Corrections Independent Review Panel, a body appointed by the Governor and composed of correctional consultants and representatives from state agencies, concluded that California's prisons are " 'severely overcrowded, imperiling the safety of both correctional employees and inmates.' "[1] Juris. Statement App., O. T. 2009, No. 09–416,

---

1. A similar conclusion was reached by the Little Hoover Commission, a bipartisan and independent state body, which stated that "[o]vercrowded conditions inside the prison walls are unsafe for inmates and staff," Solving California's Corrections Crisis: Time is Running Out 17 (Jan. 2007), and that "California's correctional system is in a tailspin," *id.*, at i. At trial, current and former California prison officials also testified to the degree of overcrowding. Jeanne Woodford, who recently administered California's prison system, stated that " '[o]vercrowding in the [California Department of Corrections and Rehabilitation (CDCR)] is extreme, its effects are pervasive and it is preventing the Department from providing adequate mental and medical health care to prisoners.' " Juris. App. 84a. Matthew Cate, the head of the California prison system, stated that " 'overpopulation makes everything we do more difficult.' " *Ibid.* And Robin Dezember, chief deputy secretary of Correctional Healthcare Services, stated that "we are terribly overcrowded in our prison system" and "overcrowding has negative effects on everybody in the prison system." Tr. 853, 856. Experts from outside California offered similar assessments. Doyle Wayne Scott, the former head of corrections in Texas, described conditions in California's prisons as "appalling," "inhumane," and "unacceptable" and stated that "[i]n more than 35 years of prison work experience, I have never seen anything like it." App. 1337. Joseph Lehman, the former head of correctional systems in Washington, Maine, and Pennsylvania, concluded that "[t]here is no question that California's

p. 56a (hereinafter Juris. App.). In 2006, then-Governor Schwarzenegger declared a state of emergency in the prisons, as "'immediate action is necessary to prevent death and harm caused by California's severe prison overcrowding.'" *Id.*, at 61a. The consequences of overcrowding identified by the Governor include "'increased, substantial risk for transmission of infectious illness'" and a suicide rate "'approaching an average of one per week.'" *Ibid.*

Prisoners in California with serious mental illness do not receive minimal, adequate care. Because of a shortage of treatment beds, suicidal inmates may be held for prolonged periods in telephone-booth sized cages without toilets. See Appendix C, *infra*. A psychiatric expert reported observing an inmate who had been held in such a cage for nearly 24 hours, standing in a pool of his own urine, unresponsive and nearly catatonic. Prison officials explained they had "'no place to put him.'" App. 593. Other inmates awaiting care may be held for months in administrative segregation, where they endure harsh and isolated conditions and receive only limited mental health services. Wait times for mental health care range as high as 12 months. *Id.*, at 704. In 2006, the suicide rate in California's prisons was nearly 80% higher than the national average for prison populations; and a court-appointed Special Master found that 72.1% of suicides involved "some measure of inadequate assessment, treatment, or intervention, and were therefore most probably foreseeable and/or preventable."[2] *Id.*, at 1781.

Prisoners suffering from physical illness also receive severely deficient care. California's prisons were designed to meet the medical needs of a population at 100% of design capacity and so have only

---

prisons are overcrowded" and that "this is an emergency situation; it calls for drastic and immediate action." *Id.*, at 1312.

2. At the time of the three-judge court's decision, 2006 was the most recent year for which the Special Master had conducted a detailed study of suicides in the California prisons. The Special Master later issued an analysis for the year 2007. This report concluded that the 2007 suicide rate was "a continuation of the CDCR's pattern of exceeding the national prison suicide rate." Record in No. 2:90–CV–00520–LKK–JFM (ED/ND Cal.), Doc. 3677, p. 1. The report found that the rate of suicides involving inadequate assessment, treatment, or intervention had risen to 82% and concluded that "[t]hese numbers clearly indicate no improvement in this area during the past several years, and possibly signal a trend of ongoing deterioration." *Id.*, at 12. No detailed study has been filed since then, but in September 2010 the Special Master filed a report stating that "the data for 2010 so far is not showing improvement in suicide prevention." App. 868.

half the clinical space needed to treat the current population. *Id.*, at 1024. A correctional officer testified that, in one prison, up to 50 sick inmates may be held together in a 12- by 20-foot cage for up to five hours awaiting treatment. Tr. 597–599. The number of staff is inadequate, and prisoners face significant delays in access to care. A prisoner with severe abdominal pain died after a 5-week delay in referral to a specialist; a prisoner with "constant and extreme" chest pain died after an 8-hour delay in evaluation by a doctor; and a prisoner died of testicular cancer after a "failure of MDs to work up for cancer in a young man with 17 months of testicular pain."[3] California Prison Health Care Receivership Corp., K. Imai, Analysis of CDCR Death Reviews 2006, pp. 6–7 (Aug. 2007). Doctor Ronald Shansky, former medical director of the Illinois state prison system, surveyed death reviews for California prisoners. He concluded that extreme departures from the standard of care were "widespread," Tr. 430, and that the proportion of "possibly preventable or preventable" deaths was "extremely high." *Id.*, at 429.[4] Many more prisoners, suffering from severe

---

3. Because plaintiffs do not base their case on deficiencies in care provided on any one occasion, this Court has no occasion to consider whether these instances of delay—or any other particular deficiency in medical care complained of by the plaintiffs—would violate the Constitution under *Estelle v. Gamble*, 429 U. S. 97, 104–105 (1976), if considered in isolation. Plaintiffs rely on systemwide deficiencies in the provision of medical and mental health care that, taken as a whole, subject sick and mentally ill prisoners in California to "substantial risk of serious harm" and cause the delivery of care in the prisons to fall below the evolving standards of decency that mark the progress of a maturing society. *Farmer v. Brennan*, 511 U. S. 825, 834 (1994)

4 In 2007, the last year for which the three-judge court had available statistics, an analysis of deaths in California's prisons found 68 preventable or possibly preventable deaths. California Prison Health Care Receivership Corp., K. Imai, Analysis of Year 2007 Death Reviews 18 (Nov. 2008). This was essentially unchanged from 2006, when an analysis found 66 preventable or possibly preventable deaths. Ibid. These statistics mean that, during 2006 and 2007, a preventable or possibly preventable death occurred once every five to six days. Both preventable and possibly preventable deaths involve major lapses in medical care and are a serious cause for concern. In one typical case classified as a possibly preventable death, an analysis revealed the following lapses: "16 month delay in evaluating abnormal liver mass; 8 month delay in receiving regular chemotherapy ... ; multiple providers fail to respond to jaundice and abnormal liver function tests causing 17 month delay in diagnosis." California Prison Health Care Receivership Corp., K. Imai, Analysis of Year 2009 Inmate Death Reviews—California Prison Health Care System 12 (Sept. 2010) (hereinafter 2009 Death Reviews). The three-judge court did not have access to statistics for 2008, but in that year the number of preventable or possibly preventable deaths held steady at 66. California Prison Health Care Receivership Corp., K. Imai, Analysis of Year 2008 Death Reviews 9 (Dec. 2009). In 2009, the number of preventable or possibly preventable deaths dropped to 46. 2009 Death Reviews 11, 13. The three-judge court

but not life-threatening conditions, experience prolonged illness and unnecessary pain....

II

As a consequence of their own actions, prisoners may be deprived of rights that are fundamental to liberty. Yet the law and the Constitution demand recognition of certain other rights. Prisoners retain the essence of human dignity inherent in all persons. Respect for that dignity animates the Eighth Amendment prohibition against cruel and unusual punishment. " 'The basic concept underlying the Eighth Amendment is nothing less than the dignity of man.' " *Atkins v. Virginia*, 536 U. S. 304, 311 (2002) (quoting *Trop v. Dulles*, 356 U. S. 86, 100 (1958) (plurality opinion)).

To incarcerate, society takes from prisoners the means to provide for their own needs. Prisoners are dependent on the State for food, clothing, and necessary medical care. A prison's failure to provide sustenance for inmates "may actually produce physical 'torture or a lingering death.' " *Estelle v. Gamble*, 429 U. S. 97, 103 (1976) (quoting *In re Kemmler*, 136 U. S. 436, 447 (1890)); see generally A. Elsner, Gates of Injustice: The Crisis in America's Prisons (2004). Just as a prisoner may starve if not fed, he or she may suffer or die if not provided adequate medical care. A prison that deprives prisoners of basic sustenance, including adequate medical care, is incompatible with the concept of human dignity and has no place in civilized society.

If government fails to fulfill this obligation, the courts have a responsibility to remedy the resulting Eighth Amendment violation. See *Hutto v. Finney*, 437 U. S. 678, 687, n. 9 (1978) . Courts must be sensitive to the State's interest in punishment, deterrence, and rehabilitation, as well as the need for deference to experienced and expert prison administrators faced with the difficult and dangerous task of housing large numbers of convicted criminals. See *Bell v. Wolfish*, 441 U. S. 520, 547–548 (1979) . Courts nevertheless must not shrink from their obligation to "enforce the constitutional rights of all 'persons,'

---

could not have anticipated this development, and it would be inappropriate for this Court to evaluate its significance for the first time on appeal. The three-judge court should, of course, consider this and any other evidence of improved conditions when considering future requests by the State for modification of its order. See infra, at 45–48.

including prisoners." *Cruz v. Beto*, 405 U. S. 319, 321 (1972) (per curiam). Courts may not allow constitutional violations to continue simply because a remedy would involve intrusion into the realm of prison administration....

A

The State contends that it was error to convene the three-judge court without affording it more time to comply with the prior orders in *Coleman* and *Plata*....

2

...Having engaged in remedial efforts for 5 years in *Plata* and 12 in *Coleman*, the District Courts were not required to wait to see whether their more recent efforts would yield equal disappointment. When a court attempts to remedy an entrenched constitutional violation through reform of a complex institution, such as this statewide prison system, it may be necessary in the ordinary course to issue multiple orders directing and adjusting ongoing remedial efforts. Each new order must be given a reasonable time to succeed, but reasonableness must be assessed in light of the entire history of the court's remedial efforts. A contrary reading of the reasonable time requirement would in effect require district courts to impose a moratorium on new remedial orders before issuing a population limit. This unnecessary period of inaction would delay an eventual remedy and would prolong the courts' involvement, serving neither the State nor the prisoners. Congress did not require this unreasonable result when it used the term "reasonable."

The *Coleman* and *Plata* courts had a solid basis to doubt that additional efforts to build new facilities and hire new staff would achieve a remedy. Indeed, although 5 years have now passed since the appointment of the *Plata* Receiver and approval of the revised plan of action in *Coleman*, there is no indication that the constitutional violations have been cured. A report filed by the *Coleman* Special Master in July 2009 describes ongoing violations, including an "absence of timely access to appropriate levels of care at every point in the system." App. 807. A report filed by the *Plata* Receiver in October 2010 likewise describes ongoing deficiencies in the provision of medical care and concludes that there are simply "too many prisoners for the healthcare infrastructure." *Id.*, at 1655. The *Coleman* and *Plata* courts acted reasonably when they convened a three-judge court without further delay.

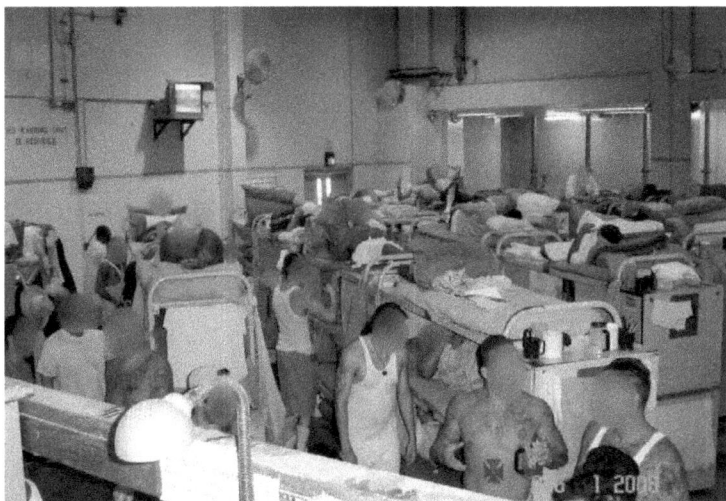

Mule Creek State Prison
Aug. 1, 2008

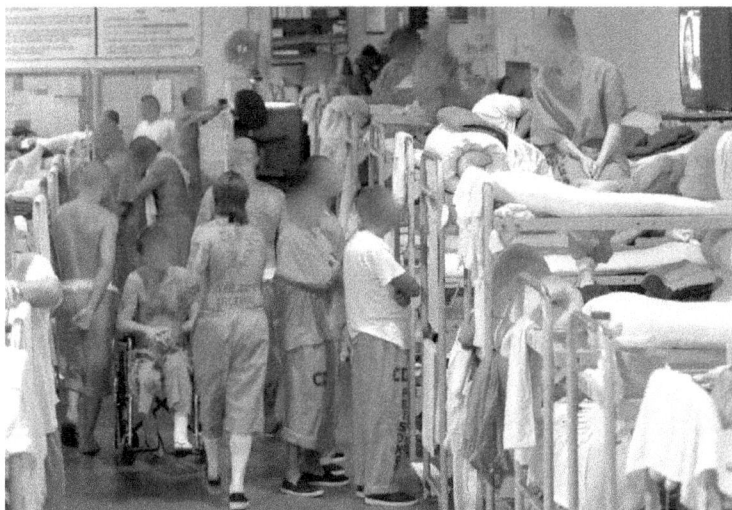

California Institution for Men
Aug. 7, 2006

C

Salinas Valley State Prison
July 29, 2008

Correctional Treatment Center (dry cages/holding cells for people waiting for mental health crisis bed)

JUSTICE SCALIA, with whom **JUSTICE THOMAS** joins, dissenting.

Today the Court affirms what is perhaps the most radical injunction issued by a court in our Nation's history: an order requiring California to release the staggering number of 46,000 convicted criminals.

There comes before us, now and then, a case whose proper outcome is so clearly indicated by tradition and common sense, that its decision ought to shape the law, rather than vice versa. One would think that, before allowing the decree of a federal district court to release 46,000 convicted felons, this Court would bend every effort to read the law in such a way as to avoid that outrageous result. Today, quite to the contrary, the Court disregards stringently drawn provisions of the governing statute, and traditional constitutional limitations upon the power of a federal judge, in order to uphold the absurd.

The proceedings that led to this result were a judicial travesty. I dissent because the institutional reform the District Court has undertaken violates the terms of the governing statute, ignores bedrock limitations on the power of Article III judges, and takes federal courts wildly beyond their institutional capacity.....

III

...I will state my approach briefly: In my view, a court may not order a prisoner's release unless it determines that the prisoner is suffering from a violation of his constitutional rights, and that his release, and no other relief, will remedy that violation. Thus, if the court determines that a particular prisoner is being denied constitutionally required medical treatment, and the release of that prisoner (and no other remedy) would enable him to obtain medical treatment, then the court can order his release; but a court may not order the release of prisoners who have suffered no violations of their constitutional rights, merely to make it less likely that that will happen to them in the future....

[Dissenting opinion by Justice Alito, joined by Chief Justice Roberts, omitted.]

SUPREME COURT OF THE UNITED STATES

JASON PEPPER, PETITIONER v. UNITED STATES
(562 U.S. 476)

Argued: December 6, 2010.
Decided: March 2, 2011.

JUSTICE SOTOMAYOR delivered the opinion of the Court.
This Court has long recognized that sentencing judges "exercise a wide discretion" in the types of evidence they may consider when imposing sentence and that "[h]ighly relevant—if not essential—to [the] selection of an appropriate sentence is the possession of the fullest information possible concerning the defendant's life and characteristics." *Williams v. New York*, 337 U. S. 241, 246–247 (1949). Congress codified this principle at 18 U.S.C. §3661, which provides that "[n]o limitation shall be placed on the information" a sentencing court may consider "concerning the [defendant's] background, character, and conduct," and at §3553(a), which sets forth certain factors that sentencing courts must consider, including "the history and characteristics of the defendant," §3553(a)(1). The United States Court of Appeals for the Eighth Circuit concluded in this case that the District Court, when resentencing petitioner after his initial sentence had been set aside on appeal, could not consider evidence of petitioner's rehabilitation since his initial sentencing. That conclusion conflicts with longstanding principles of federal sentencing law and Congress' express directives in §§3661 and 3553(a). Although a separate statutory provision, §3742(g)(2), prohibits a district court at resentencing from

imposing a sentence outside the Federal Sentencing Guidelines range except upon a ground it relied upon at the prior sentencing—thus effectively precluding the court from considering postsentencing rehabilitation for purposes of imposing a non-Guidelines sentence—that provision did not survive our holding in *United States v. Booker*, 543 U. S. 220 (2005), and we expressly invalidate it today.

We hold that when a defendant's sentence has been set aside on appeal, a district court at resentencing may consider evidence of the defendant's postsentencing rehabilitation and that such evidence may, in appropriate cases, support a downward variance from the now-advisory Federal Sentencing Guidelines range....

I

In October 2003, petitioner Jason Pepper was arrested and charged with conspiracy to distribute 500 grams or more of methamphetamine in violation of 21 U.S.C. §846. After pleading guilty, Pepper appeared for sentencing before then-Chief Judge Mark W. Bennett of the U. S. District Court for the Northern District of Iowa. Pepper's sentencing range under the Guidelines was 97 to 121 months.[1] The Government moved for a downward departure pursuant to USSG §5K1.1 based on Pepper's substantial assistance and recommended a 15 percent downward departure.[2] The District Court, however, sentenced Pepper to a 24-month prison term, resulting in an approximately 75 percent downward departure from the low end of the Guidelines range, to be followed by five years of supervised release. The Government appealed Pepper's sentence, and in June 2005, the Court of Appeals for the Eighth Circuit reversed and remanded for resentencing in light of our intervening decision in *Booker* (and for another reason not relevant here). See *United States v. Pepper*, 412 F. 3d 995, 999 (2005) (Pepper I).

---

1. Although the charge to which Pepper pleaded guilty carried a mandatory minimum of 120 months' imprisonment, the mandatory minimum did not apply because he was eligible for safety-valve relief pursuant to 18 U.S.C. §3553(f) (2000 ed.) and §5C1.2 of the United States Sentencing Guidelines Manual (Nov. 2003) (USSG).

2. USSG §5K1.1 provides that a court may depart from the Guidelines "[u]pon motion of the government stating that the defendant has provided substantial assistance in the investigation or prosecution of another person who has committed an offense." Pepper provided information to Government investigators and a grand jury concerning two other individuals involved with illegal drugs and guns.

Pepper completed his 24-month sentence three days after Pepper I was issued and began serving his term of supervised release.

In May 2006, the District Court conducted a resentencing hearing and heard from three witnesses. In his testimony, Pepper first recounted that while he had previously been a drug addict, he successfully completed a 500-hour drug treatment program while in prison and he no longer used any drugs. App. 104–105. Pepper then explained that since his release from prison, he had enrolled at a local community college as a full-time student and had earned A's in all of his classes in the prior semester. *Id.*, at 106–107. Pepper also testified that he had obtained employment within a few weeks after being released from custody and was continuing to work part-time while attending school. *Id.*, at 106–110. Pepper confirmed that he was in compliance with all the conditions of his supervised release and described his changed attitude since his arrest. See *id.*, at 111 ("[M]y life was basically headed to either where—I guess where I ended up, in prison, or death. Now I have some optimism about my life, about what I can do with my life. I'm glad that I got this chance to try again I guess you could say at a decent life.... My life was going nowhere before, and I think it's going somewhere now").

Pepper's father testified that he had virtually no contact with Pepper during the 5-year period leading up to his arrest. *Id.*, at 117. Pepper's drug treatment program, according to his father, "truly sobered him up" and "made his way of thinking change." *Id.*, at 121. He explained that Pepper was now "much more mature" and "serious in terms of planning for the future," *id.*, at 119, and that as a consequence, he had re-established a relationship with his son, *id.*, at 118–119.

Finally, Pepper's probation officer testified that, in his view, a 24-month sentence would be reasonable in light of Pepper's substantial assistance, postsentencing rehabilitation, and demonstrated low risk of recidivism. *Id.*, at 126–131. The probation officer also prepared a sentencing memorandum that further set forth the reasons supporting his recommendation for a 24-month sentence.

The District Court adopted as its findings of fact the testimony of the three witnesses and the probation officer's sentencing memorandum. The court granted a 40 percent downward departure based on Pepper's substantial assistance, reducing the bottom of the Guidelines range from 97 to 58 months. The court then granted a further 59 percent downward variance based on, inter alia, Pepper's rehabilitation since his initial sentencing. *Id.*, at 143–148.[3] The court sentenced Pepper to 24 months of imprisonment, concluding that "it would [not] advance any purpose of federal sentencing policy or any other policy behind the federal sentencing guidelines to send this defendant back to prison." *Id.*, at 149–150.

The Government again appealed Pepper's sentence, and the Court of Appeals again reversed and remanded for resentencing. See *United States v. Pepper*, 486 F. 3d 408, 410, 413 (CA8 2007) (*Pepper II*). The court concluded that, while it was "a close call, [it could not] say the district court abused its discretion" by granting the 40 percent downward departure for substantial assistance. *Id.*, at 411. The court found the further 59 percent downward variance, however, to be an abuse of discretion. *Id.*, at 412–413. In doing so, the court held that Pepper's "post-sentencing rehabilitation was an impermissible factor to consider in granting a downward variance." *Id.*, at 413. The court stated that evidence of postsentencing rehabilitation " 'is not relevant and will not be permitted at resentencing because the district court could not have considered that evidence at the time of the original sentencing,' " and permitting courts to consider post-sentencing rehabilitation at resentencing "would create unwarranted sentencing disparities and inject blatant inequities into the sentencing process." *Ibid.*[4] The Court of Appeals directed that the case be assigned to a different district judge for resentencing. Ibid.

After the Court of Appeals' mandate issued, Pepper's case was reassigned on remand to Chief Judge Linda R. Reade. In July 2007, Chief Judge Reade issued an order on the scope of the remand from *Pepper II*, stating that "[t]he court will not consider itself bound to re-

---

3. The court also cited Pepper's lack of a violent history and, to a lesser extent, the need to avoid unwarranted sentencing disparity with Pepper's co-conspirators. App. 144–145.

4. The Court of Appeals also held that the District Court "further erred by considering Pepper's lack of violent history, which history had already been accounted for in the sentencing Guidelines calculation, and by considering sentencing disparity among Pepper's co-defendants without adequate foundation and explanation." Pepper II, 486 F. 3d, at 413.

duce [Pepper's] advisory Sentencing Guidelines range by 40% pursuant to USSG §5K1.1." *United States v. Pepper*, No. 03–CR–4113–LRR, 2007 WL 2076041, *4 (ND Iowa 2007). In the meantime, Pepper petitioned this Court for a writ of certiorari, and in January 2008, we granted the petition, vacated the judgment in *Pepper II*, and remanded the case to the Court of Appeals for further consideration in light of *Gall v. United States*, 552 U. S. 38 (2007). See *Pepper v. United States*, 552 U.S. 1089 (2008).

On remand, the Court of Appeals held that *Gall* did not alter its prior conclusion that "post-sentence rehabilitation is an impermissible factor to consider in granting a downward variance." 518 F. 3d 949, 953 (CA8 2008) (*Pepper III*). The court again reversed the sentence and remanded for resentencing.

In October 2008, Chief Judge Reade convened Pepper's second resentencing hearing. Pepper informed the court that he was still attending school and was now working as a supervisor for the night crew at a warehouse retailer, where he was recently selected by management as "associate of the year" and was likely to be promoted the following January. App. 320, 323. Pepper also stated that he had recently married and was now supporting his wife and her daughter. *Id.*, at 321. Pepper's father reiterated that Pepper was moving forward in both his career and his family life and that he remained in close touch with his son. See *id.*, at 300–304.

In December 2008, Chief Judge Reade issued a sentencing memorandum. Noting that the remand language of *Pepper III* was nearly identical to the language in *Pepper II*, the court again observed that it was "not bound to reduce [Pepper's] advisory Sentencing Guidelines range by 40%" for substantial assistance and concluded that Pepper was entitled only to a 20 percent downward departure because the assistance was "timely, helpful and important" but "in no way extraordinary." Sealed Sentencing Memorandum in No. 03–CR–4113–LRR (ND Iowa), Doc. 198, pp. 7, 10. The court also rejected Pepper's request for a downward variance based on, inter alia, his postsentencing rehabilitation. *Id.*, at 16.

The District Court reconvened Pepper's resentencing hearing in January 2009. The court's decision to grant a 20 percent downward departure for substantial assistance resulted in an advisory Guidelines range of 77 to 97 months. The court also granted the Government's motion under Rule 35(b) of the Federal Rules of Criminal Procedure to account for investigative assistance Pepper provided after he was initially sentenced. The court imposed a 65-month term of imprisonment, to be followed by 12 months of supervised release.[5]

The Court of Appeals affirmed Pepper's 65-month sentence. 570 F. 3d 958 (CA8 2009) (*Pepper IV*). As relevant here, the Court of Appeals rejected Pepper's argument that the District Court erred in refusing to consider his postsentencing rehabilitation. The court acknowledged that "Pepper made significant progress during and following his initial period of imprisonment" and "commend[ed] Pepper on the positive changes he has made in his life," but concluded that Pepper's argument was foreclosed by Circuit precedent holding that "post-sentencing rehabilitation is not a permissible factor to consider in granting a downward variance." *Id.*, at 964–965 (citing *United States v. Jenners*, 473 F. 3d 894, 899 (CA8 2007); *United States v. McMannus*, 496 F. 3d 846, 852, n. 4 (CA8 2007))....

II

A

"It has been uniform and constant in the federal judicial tradition for the sentencing judge to consider every convicted person as an individual and every case as a unique study in the human failings that sometimes mitigate, sometimes magnify, the crime and the punishment to ensue." *Koon v. United States*, 518 U. S. 81, 113 (1996). Underlying this tradition is the principle that "the punishment should fit the offender and not merely the crime." *Williams*, 337 U. S., at 247; see also *Pennsylvania ex rel. Sullivan v. Ashe*, 302 U. S. 51, 55 (1937) ("For the determination of sentences, justice generally requires consideration of more than the particular acts by which the crime was committed and that

---

5. After the District Court resentenced Pepper to 65 months' imprisonment, Pepper was returned to federal custody. On July 22, 2010, after we granted Pepper's petition for a writ of certiorari, the District Court granted his motion for release pending disposition of the case here.

there be taken into account the circumstances of the offense together with the character and propensities of the offender").

Consistent with this principle, we have observed that "both before and since the American colonies became a nation, courts in this country and in England practiced a policy under which a sentencing judge could exercise a wide discretion in the sources and types of evidence used to assist him in determining the kind and extent of punishment to be imposed within limits fixed by law." *Williams*, 337 U. S., at 246. In particular, we have emphasized that "[h]ighly relevant—if not essential—to [the] selection of an appropriate sentence is the possession of the fullest information possible concerning the defendant's life and characteristics." *Id.*, at 247. Permitting sentencing courts to consider the widest possible breadth of information about a defendant "ensures that the punishment will suit not merely the offense but the individual defendant." *Wasman v. United States*, 468 U. S. 559, 564 (1984).

In 1970, Congress codified the "longstanding principle that sentencing courts have broad discretion to consider various kinds of information" at 18 U.S.C. §3577 (1970 ed.). *United States v. Watts*, 519 U. S. 148, 151 (1997) (per curiam). Section 3577 (1970 ed.) provided:

> No limitation shall be placed on the information concerning the background, character, and conduct of a person convicted of an offense which a court of the United States may receive and consider for the purpose of imposing an appropriate sentence." (Emphasis added.)

In the Sentencing Reform Act of 1984 (SRA), 18 U.S.C. §3551 *et seq.*, Congress effected fundamental changes to federal sentencing by creating the Federal Sentencing Commission and introducing the Guidelines scheme. In doing so, however, Congress recodified §3577 without change at §3661. The Sentencing Commission, moreover, expressly incorporated §3661 in the Guidelines:

> In determining the sentence to impose within the guideline range, or whether a departure from the guidelines is warranted, the court may consider, *without limitation*, any information concerning the background, character and conduct of the defendant, unless otherwise prohibited by law. See 18 U.S.C. §3661." USSG §1B1.4 (2010) (emphasis added).

Both Congress and the Sentencing Commission thus expressly preserved the traditional discretion of sentencing courts to "conduct an inquiry broad in scope, largely unlimited either as to the kind of information [they] may consider, or the source from which it may come." *United States v. Tucker*, 404 U. S. 443, 446 (1972). [8]

The SRA did constrain sentencing courts' discretion in important respects, most notably by making the Guidelines mandatory, see 18 U.S.C. §3553(b)(1) (2000 ed., Supp. IV), and by specifying various factors that courts must consider in exercising their discretion, see §3553(a). In our seminal decision in *Booker*, we held that where facts found by a judge by a preponderance of the evidence increased the applicable Guidelines range, treating the Guidelines as mandatory in those circumstances violated the Sixth Amendment right of criminal defendants to be tried by a jury and to have every element of an offense proved by the Government beyond a reasonable doubt. 543 U. S., at 243–244. Our remedial opinion in *Booker* invalidated two offending provisions in the SRA, see *id.*, at 245 (invalidating 18 U.S.C. §§3553(b)(1)), and instructed the district courts to treat the Guidelines as "effectively advisory," 543 U.S., at 245.

Our post-*Booker* opinions make clear that, although a sentencing court must "give respectful consideration to the Guidelines, *Booker* permits the court to tailor the sentence in light of other statutory concerns as well." *Kimbrough v. United States*, 552 U. S. 85, 101 (2007) (internal quotation marks and citation omitted). Accordingly, although the "Guidelines should be the starting point and the initial benchmark," district courts may impose sentences within statutory limits based on appropriate consideration of all of the factors listed in §3553(a), subject to appellate review for "reasonableness." *Gall*, 552 U. S., at 49–51. This sentencing framework applies both at a defendant's initial sentencing and at any subsequent resentencing after a sentence has been set aside on appeal. See 18 U.S.C. §3742(g) ("A district court to which a case is remanded...shall resentence a defendant in accordance with section 3553"); see also *Dillon v. United States*, 560 U. S. 817, 827 (2010) (distinguishing between "sentence-modification proceedings" under 18 U.S.C. §3582(c)(2), which "do not implicate the in-

8. Of course, sentencing courts' discretion under §3661 is subject to constitutional constraints. See, e.g., *United States v. Leung*, 40 F. 3d 577, 586 (CA2 1994) ("A defendant's race or nationality may play no adverse role in the administration of justice, including at sentencing").

terests identified in *Booker*," and "plenary resentencing proceedings," which do).

B

In light of the federal sentencing framework described above, we think it clear that when a defendant's sentence has been set aside on appeal and his case remanded for resentencing, a district court may consider evidence of a defendant's rehabilitation since his prior sentencing and that such evidence may, in appropriate cases, support a downward variance from the advisory Guidelines range....

As the original sentencing judge recognized, the extensive evidence of Pepper's rehabilitation since his initial sentencing is clearly relevant to the selection of an appropriate sentence in this case. Most fundamentally, evidence of Pepper's conduct since his release from custody in June 2005 provides the most up-to-date picture of Pepper's "history and characteristics." §3553(a)(1); see *United States v. Bryson*, 229 F. 3d 425, 426 (CA2 2000) ("[A] court's duty is always to sentence the defendant as he stands before the court on the day of sentencing"). At the time of his initial sentencing in 2004, Pepper was a 25-year-old drug addict who was unemployed, estranged from his family, and had recently sold drugs as part of a methamphetamine conspiracy. By the time of his second resentencing in 2009, Pepper had been drug-free for nearly five years, had attended college and achieved high grades, was a top employee at his job slated for a promotion, had re-established a relationship with his father, and was married and supporting his wife's daughter. There is no question that this evidence of Pepper's conduct since his initial sentencing constitutes a critical part of the "history and characteristics" of a defendant that Congress intended sentencing courts to consider. §3553(a).

Pepper's postsentencing conduct also sheds light on the likelihood that he will engage in future criminal conduct, a central factor that district courts must assess when imposing sentence. See §§3553(a)(2)(B)–(C); *Gall*, 552 U. S., at 59 ("Gall's self-motivated rehabilitation …lends strong support to the conclusion that imprisonment was not necessary to deter Gall from engaging in future criminal conduct or to protect the public from his future criminal acts" (citing §§3553(a)

(2)(B)–(C))). As recognized by Pepper's probation officer, Pepper's steady employment, as well as his successful completion of a 500-hour drug treatment program and his drug-free condition, also suggest a diminished need for "educational or vocational training...or other correctional treatment." §3553(a)(2)(D). Finally, Pepper's exemplary postsentencing conduct may be taken as the most accurate indicator of "his present purposes and tendencies and significantly to suggest the period of restraint and the kind of discipline that ought to be imposed upon him." *Ashe*, 302 U. S., at 55. Accordingly, evidence of Pepper's postsentencing rehabilitation bears directly on the District Court's overarching duty to "impose a sentence sufficient, but not greater than necessary" to serve the purposes of sentencing. §3553(a).

In sum, the Court of Appeals' ruling prohibiting the District Court from considering any evidence of Pepper's postsentencing rehabilitation at resentencing conflicts with longstanding principles of federal sentencing law and contravenes Congress' directives in §§3661 and 3553(a)....

JUSTICE THOMAS, dissenting.

I would affirm the Court of Appeals and uphold Pepper's sentence. As written, the Federal Sentencing Guidelines do not permit district courts to impose a sentence below the Guidelines range based on the defendant's postsentencing rehabilitation.[1] See United States Sentencing Commission, Guidelines Manual §5K2.19 (Nov. 2010) (USSG). Therefore, I respectfully dissent.

In *United States v. Booker*, 543 U. S. 220, 258–265 (2005), the Court rendered the entire Guidelines scheme advisory, a remedy that was "far broader than necessary to correct constitutional error." *Kimbrough v. United States*, 552 U. S. 85, 114 (2007) (Thomas, J. , dissenting). Because there is "no principled way to apply the *Booker* remedy," I have explained that it is "best to apply the statute as written, including 18 U.S.C. §3553(b), which makes the Guidelines mandatory," unless doing

---

1. I agree with the Court that the law of the case doctrine did not control Pepper's resentencing. [Citation omitted].

so would actually violate the Sixth Amendment. *Id.*, at 116; see *Booker*, supra, at 313–326 (Thomas , J., dissenting in part); *Gall v. United States*, 552 U. S. 38, 61 (2007) (Thomas , J., dissenting); *Irizarry v. United States*, 553 U. S. 708, 717 (2008) (Thomas, J., concurring).

I would apply the Guidelines as written in this case because doing so would not violate the Sixth Amendment. The constitutional problem arises only when a judge makes "a finding that raises the sentence beyond the sentence that could have lawfully been imposed by reference to facts found by the jury or admitted by the defendant." *Booker*, supra, at 313 (opinion of Thomas , J.). Pepper admitted in his plea agreement to involvement with between 1,500 and 5,000 grams of methamphetamine mixture, which carries a sentence of 10 years to life under 21 U.S.C. §841(b)(1)(A)(viii).[2] *United States v. Pepper*, 412 F. 3d 995, 996 (CA8 2005). Because Pepper has admitted facts that would support a much longer sentence than the 65 months he received, there is no Sixth Amendment problem in this case.

Under a mandatory Guidelines regime, Pepper's sentence was proper. The District Court correctly calculated the Guidelines range, incorporated a USSG §5K1.1 departure and the Government's motion under Federal Rule of Criminal Procedure 35(b), and settled on a 65-month sentence. Guideline §5K2.19 expressly prohibits downward departures based on "[p]ost-sentencing rehabilitative efforts, even if exceptional." Nor is there any provision in the Guidelines for the "variance" Pepper seeks, as such variances are creations of the Booker remedy. I would therefore affirm the Court of Appeals' decision to uphold Pepper's sentence.

Although this outcome would not represent my own policy choice, I am bound by the choices made by Congress and the Federal Sentencing Commission. Like the majority, I believe that postsentencing rehabilitation can be highly relevant to meaningful resentencing. [Citation omitted.] In light of Pepper's success in escaping drug addiction and becoming a productive member of society, I do not see what purpose further incarceration would serve. But Congress made the Guidelines mandatory, see 18 U.S.C. §3553(b)(1), and authorized USSG §5K2.19.

---

2. Pepper also stated that he understood both the 10-year statutory minimum and that the Government was making no promises about any exceptions.

I am constrained to apply those provisions unless the Constitution prohibits me from doing so, and it does not here.

[Partial concurrence by Justice Breyer and partial concurrence and dissent by Justice Alito are omitted. Justice Kagan took no part in this case."

SUPREME COURT OF THE UNITED STATES

MILLER v. ALABAMA
(567 U.S. 460)

Argued: March 20, 2012.
Decided: June 25, 2012.

JUSTICE KAGAN delivered the opinion of the Court.

The two 14-year-old offenders in these cases were convicted of murder and sentenced to life imprisonment without the possibility of parole. In neither case did the sentencing authority have any discretion to impose a different punishment. State law mandated that each juvenile die in prison even if a judge or jury would have thought that his youth and its attendant characteristics, along with the nature of his crime, made a lesser sentence (for example, life with the possibility of parole) more appropriate. Such a scheme prevents those meting out punishment from considering a juvenile's "lessened culpability" and greater "capacity for change," *Graham v. Florida*, 560 U. S. 48, 68, 74 (2010), and runs afoul of our cases' requirement of individualized sentencing for defendants facing the most serious penalties. We therefore hold that mandatory life without parole for those under the age of 18 at the time of their crimes violates the Eighth Amendment's prohibition on "cruel and unusual punishments."

I
A

In November 1999, petitioner Kuntrell Jackson, then 14 years old, and two other boys decided to rob a video store. En route to the store,

Jackson learned that one of the boys, Derrick Shields, was carrying a sawed-off shotgun in his coat sleeve. Jackson decided to stay outside when the two other boys entered the store. Inside, Shields pointed the gun at the store clerk, Laurie Troup, and demanded that she "give up the money." *Jackson v. State*, 359 Ark. 87, 89, 194 S. W. 3d 757, 759 (2004) (internal quotation marks omitted). Troup refused. A few moments later, Jackson went into the store to find Shields continuing to demand money. At trial, the parties disputed whether Jackson warned Troup that "[w]e ain't playin'," or instead told his friends, "I thought you all was playin'." *Id.*, at 91, 194 S. W. 3d, at 760 (internal quotation marks omitted). When Troup threatened to call the police, Shields shot and killed her. The three boys fled empty-handed. See *id.*, at 89-92, 194 S. W. 3d, at 758-760.

Arkansas law gives prosecutors discretion to charge 14-year-olds as adults when they are alleged to have committed certain serious offenses. See Ark. Code Ann. §9-27-318(c)(2) (1998). The prosecutor here exercised that authority by charging Jackson with capital felony murder and aggravated robbery. Jackson moved to transfer the case to juvenile court, but after considering the alleged facts of the crime, a psychiatrist's examination, and Jackson's juvenile arrest history (shoplifting and several incidents of car theft), the trial court denied the motion, and an appellate court affirmed. See *Jackson v. State*, No. 02-535, 2003 WL 193412, *1 (Ark. App., Jan. 29, 2003); §§9-27-318(d), (e). A jury later convicted Jackson of both crimes. Noting that "in view of [the] verdict, there's only one possible punishment," the judge sentenced Jackson to life without parole. App. in No. 10-9647, p. 55 (hereinafter Jackson App.); see Ark. Code Ann. §5-4-104(b) (1997) ("A defendant convicted of capital murder or treason shall be sentenced to death or life imprisonment without parole").[1] Jackson did not challenge the sentence on appeal, and the Arkansas Supreme Court affirmed the convictions. See 359 Ark. 87, 194 S. W. 3d 757.

Following *Roper v. Simmons*, 543 U. S. 551 (2005), in which this Court invalidated the death penalty for all juvenile offenders under the

---

[1]. Jackson was ineligible for the death penalty under *Thompson v. Oklahoma*, 487 U. S. 815 (1988) (plurality opinion), which held that capital punishment of offenders under the age of 16 violates the Eighth Amendment.

age of 18, Jackson filed a state petition for habeas corpus. He argued, based on *Roper*'s reasoning, that a mandatory sentence of life without parole for a 14-year-old also violates the Eighth Amendment. The circuit court rejected that argument and granted the State's motion to dismiss. See Jackson App. 72-76. While that ruling was on appeal, this Court held in *Graham v. Florida* that life without parole violates the Eighth Amendment when imposed on juvenile nonhomicide offenders. After the parties filed briefs addressing that decision, the Arkansas Supreme Court affirmed the dismissal of Jackson's petition. See *Jackson v. Norris*, 378 S. W. 3d, 103. The majority found that Roper and Graham were "narrowly tailored" to their contexts: "death-penalty cases involving a juvenile and life-imprisonment-without-parole cases for nonhomicide offenses involving a juvenile." *Id.*, at 5, 378 S. W. 3d, at 106. Two justices dissented. They noted that Jackson was not the shooter and that "any evidence of intent to kill was severely lacking." *Id.*, at 10, 378 S. W. 3d, at 109 (Danielson, J., dissenting). And they argued that Jackson's mandatory sentence ran afoul of Graham's admonition that " '[a]n offender's age is relevant to the Eighth Amendment, and criminal procedure laws that fail to take defendants' youthfulness into account at all would be flawed.' " *Id.*, at 10-11, 378 S. W. 3d, at 109 (quoting *Graham*, 560 U. S., at 76).[2]

B

Like Jackson, petitioner Evan Miller was 14 years old at the time of his crime. Miller had by then been in and out of foster care because his mother suffered from alcoholism and drug addiction and his stepfather abused him. Miller, too, regularly used drugs and alcohol; and he had attempted suicide four times, the first when he was six years old. See *E. J. M. v. State*, 928 So. 2d 1077, 1081 (Ala. Crim. App. 2004) (Cobb,

---

2. For the first time in this Court, Arkansas contends that Jackson's sentence was not mandatory. On its view, state law then in effect allowed the trial judge to suspend the life-without-parole sentence and commit Jackson to the Department of Human Services for a "training-school program," at the end of which he could be placed on probation. Brief for Respondent in No. 10-9647, pp. 36-37 (hereinafter Arkansas Brief) (citing Ark. Code Ann. §12-28-403(b)(2) (1999)). But Arkansas never raised that objection in the state courts, and they treated Jackson's sentence as mandatory. We abide by that interpretation of state law. See, e.g., *Mullaney v. Wilbur*, 421 U. S. 684, 690-691 (1975).

J., concurring in result); App. in No. 10-9646, pp. 26-28 (hereinafter Miller App.).

One night in 2003, Miller was at home with a friend, Colby Smith, when a neighbor, Cole Cannon, came to make a drug deal with Miller's mother. See 6 Record in No. 10-9646, p. 1004. The two boys followed Cannon back to his trailer, where all three smoked marijuana and played drinking games. When Cannon passed out, Miller stole his wallet, splitting about $300 with Smith. Miller then tried to put the wallet back in Cannon's pocket, but Cannon awoke and grabbed Miller by the throat. Smith hit Cannon with a nearby baseball bat, and once released, Miller grabbed the bat and repeatedly struck Cannon with it. Miller placed a sheet over Cannon's head, told him " 'I am God, I've come to take your life,' " and delivered one more blow. *Miller v. State*, 63 So. 3d 676, 689 (Ala. Crim. App. 2010). The boys then retreated to Miller's trailer, but soon decided to return to Cannon's to cover up evidence of their crime. Once there, they lit two fires. Cannon eventually died from his injuries and smoke inhalation. See *id.*, at 683-685, 689.

Alabama law required that Miller initially be charged as a juvenile, but allowed the District Attorney to seek removal of the case to adult court. See Ala. Code §12-15-34 (1977). The D.A. did so, and the juvenile court agreed to the transfer after a hearing. Citing the nature of the crime, Miller's "mental maturity," and his prior juvenile offenses (truancy and "criminal mischief"), the Alabama Court of Criminal Appeals affirmed. *E. J. M. v. State*, No. CR-03-0915, pp. 5-7 (Aug. 27, 2004) (unpublished memorandum).[3] The State accordingly charged Miller as an adult with murder in the course of arson. That crime (like capital murder in Arkansas) carries a mandatory minimum punishment of life without parole. See Ala. Code §§13A-5-40(9), 13A-6-2(c) (1982).

---

3. The Court of Criminal Appeals also affirmed the juvenile court's denial of Miller's request for funds to hire his own mental expert for the transfer hearing. The court pointed out that under governing Alabama Supreme Court precedent, "the procedural requirements of a trial do not ordinarily apply" to those hearings. *E. J. M. v. State*, 928 So. 2d 1077 (2004) (Cobb, J., concurring in result) (internal quotation marks omitted). In a separate opinion, Judge Cobb agreed on the reigning precedent, but urged the State Supreme Court to revisit the question in light of transfer hearings' importance. See *id.*, at 1081 ("[A]lthough later mental evaluation as an adult affords some semblance of procedural due process, it is, in effect, too little, too late").

Relying in significant part on testimony from Smith, who had pleaded to a lesser offense, a jury found Miller guilty. He was therefore sentenced to life without the possibility of parole. The Alabama Court of Criminal Appeals affirmed, ruling that life without parole was "not overly harsh when compared to the crime" and that the mandatory nature of the sentencing scheme was permissible under the Eighth Amendment. 63 So. 3d, at 690; see *id.*, at 686-691. The Alabama Supreme Court denied review.

We granted certiorari in both cases, see 565 U. S. 1013 (2011) (No. 10-9646); 565 U. S. 1013 (2011) (No. 10-9647), and now reverse.

II

The Eighth Amendment's prohibition of cruel and unusual punishment "guarantees individuals the right not to be subjected to excessive sanctions." *Roper*, 543 U. S., at 560. That right, we have explained, "flows from the basic 'precept of justice that punishment for crime should be graduated and proportioned'" to both the offender and the offense. Ibid. (quoting *Weems v. United States*, 217 U. S. 349, 367 (1910)). As we noted the last time we considered life-without-parole sentences imposed on juveniles, "[t]he concept of proportionality is central to the Eighth Amendment." *Graham*, 560 U. S., at 59. And we view that concept less through a historical prism than according to "'the evolving standards of decency that mark the progress of a maturing society.'" *Estelle v. Gamble*, 429 U. S. 97, 102 (1976) (quoting *Trop v. Dulles*, 356 U. S. 86, 101 (1958) (plurality opinion)).

The cases before us implicate two strands of precedent reflecting our concern with proportionate punishment. The first has adopted categorical bans on sentencing practices based on mismatches between the culpability of a class of offenders and the severity of a penalty. See *Graham*, 560 U. S., at 60–61 (listing cases). So, for example, we have held that imposing the death penalty for nonhomicide crimes against individuals, or imposing it on mentally retarded defendants, violates the Eighth Amendment. See *Kennedy v. Louisiana*, 554 U. S. 407 (2008); *Atkins v. Virginia*, 536 U. S. 304 (2002). Several of the cases in this group have specially focused on juvenile offenders, because of their lesser culpability. Thus, *Roper* held that the Eighth Amendment bars capital punishment for children, and *Graham* concluded that the Amendment also prohibits a sentence of life without the possibility of parole for a child who committed a nonhomicide offense. *Graham* further likened life without parole for juveniles to the death penalty itself, thereby evoking a second line of our precedents. In those cases, we have prohibited mandatory imposition of capital punishment, requiring that sentencing authorities consider the characteristics of a defendant and the details of his offense before sentencing him to death. See *Woodson v. North Carolina*, 428 U. S. 280 (1976) (plurality opinion); *Lockett v. Ohio*, 438 U. S. 586 (1978). Here, the confluence of these two lines of precedent leads to the conclusion that mandatory life-without-parole sentences for juveniles violate the Eighth Amendment.[4]

To start with the first set of cases: *Roper* and *Graham* establish that children are constitutionally different from adults for purposes of sentencing. Because juveniles have diminished culpability and greater prospects for reform, we explained, "they are less deserving of the most severe punishments." *Graham*, 560 U. S., at 68. Those cases relied on three significant gaps between juveniles and adults. First, children have a " 'lack of maturity and an underdeveloped sense of responsibility,' " leading to recklessness, impulsivity, and heedless risk-taking. *Roper*, 543 U. S., at 569. Second, children "are more vulnerable...to negative influences and outside pressures," including from their family and peers; they have limited "contro[l] over their own environment" and lack the ability to extricate themselves from horrific, crime-producing

---

4 The three dissenting opinions here each take issue with some or all of those precedents. See post, at 5-6 (opinion of ROBERTS, C. J.); post, at 1-6 (opinion of THOMAS, J.); post, at 1-4 (opinion of ALITO, J.). That is not surprising: their authors (and joiner) each dissented from some or all of those precedents. See, *e.g.*, *Kennedy*, 554 U. S., at 447 (ALITO, J., joined by ROBERTS, C. J., and SCALIA and THOMAS, JJ., dissenting); *Roper*, 543 U. S., at 607 (SCALIA, J., joined by THOMAS, J., dissenting); *Atkins*, 536 U. S., at 337 (SCALIA, J., joined by THOMAS, J., dissenting); *Thompson*, 487 U. S., at 859 (SCALIA, J., dissenting); *Graham v. Collins*, 506 U. S. 461, 487 (1993) (THOMAS, J., concurring) (contending that *Woodson* was wrongly decided). In particular, each disagreed with the majority's reasoning in *Graham*, which is the foundation stone of our analysis. See *Graham*, 560 U. S., at 86 (ROBERTS, C. J., concurring in judgment); *id.*, at 97 (THOMAS, J., joined by SCALIA and ALITO, JJ., dissenting); *id.*, at 124 (ALITO, J., dissenting). While the dissents seek to relitigate old Eighth Amendment battles, repeating many arguments this Court has previously (and often) rejected, we apply the logic of *Roper*, *Graham*, and our individualized sentencing decisions to these two cases.

settings. *Ibid.* And third, a child's character is not as "well formed" as an adult's; his traits are "less fixed" and his actions less likely to be "evidence of irretrievabl[e] deprav[ity]." *Id.*, at 570.

Our decisions rested not only on common sense—on what "any parent knows"—but on science and social science as well. *Id.*, at 569. In *Roper*, we cited studies showing that "'[o]nly a relatively small proportion of adolescents'" who engage in illegal activity "'develop entrenched patterns of problem behavior.'" *Id.*, at 570 (quoting Steinberg & Scott, Less Guilty by Reason of Adolescence: Developmental Immaturity, Diminished Responsibility, and the Juvenile Death Penalty, 58 Am. Psychologist 1009, 1014 (2003)). And in *Graham*, we noted that "developments in psychology and brain science continue to show fundamental differences between juvenile and adult minds"—for example, in "parts of the brain involved in behavior control." 560 U. S., at 68.[5] We reasoned that those findings—of transient rashness, proclivity for risk, and inability to assess consequences—both lessened a child's "moral culpability" and enhanced the prospect that, as the years go by and neurological development occurs, his "'deficiencies will be reformed.'" *Id.*, at *Ibid.* (quoting *Roper*, 543 U. S., at 570).

Roper and *Graham* emphasized that the distinctive attributes of youth diminish the penological justifications for imposing the harshest sentences on juvenile offenders, even when they commit terrible crimes. Because "'[t]he heart of the retribution rationale'" relates to an offender's blameworthiness, "'the case for retribution is not as strong with a minor as with an adult.'" *Graham*, 560 U. S., at 71 (quoting *Tison v. Arizona*, 481 U. S. 137, 149 (1987); *Roper*, 543 U. S., at 571). Nor can deterrence do the work in this context, because "'the same characteristics that render juveniles less culpable than adults'"—their

5. The evidence presented to us in these cases indicates that the science and social science supporting *Roper*'s and *Graham*'s conclusions have become even stronger. See, e.g., Brief for American Psychological Association et al. as *Amici Curiae* 3 ("[A]n ever-growing body of research in developmental psychology and neuroscience continues to confirm and strengthen the Court's conclusions"); *id.*, at 4 ("It is increasingly clear that adolescent brains are not yet fully mature in regions and systems related to higher-order executive functions such as impulse control, planning ahead, and risk avoidance"); Brief for J. Lawrence Aber et al. as *Amici Curiae* 12-28 (discussing post-*Graham* studies); *id.*, at 26-27 ("Numerous studies post-*Graham* indicate that exposure to deviant peers leads to increased deviant behavior and is a consistent predictor of adolescent delinquency" (footnote omitted)).

immaturity, recklessness, and impetuosity—make them less likely to consider potential punishment. *Graham*, 560 U. S., at 72 (quoting *Roper*, 543 U. S., at 571). Similarly, incapacitation could not support the life-without-parole sentence in *Graham*: Deciding that a "juvenile offender forever will be a danger to society" would require "mak[ing] a judgment that [he] is incorrigible"—but "'incorrigibility is inconsistent with youth.'" 560 U. S., at 72–73 (quoting *Workman v. Commonwealth*, 429 S. W. 2d 374, 378 (Ky. App. 1968)). And for the same reason, rehabilitation could not justify that sentence. Life without parole "forswears altogether the rehabilitative ideal." *Graham*, 560 U. S., at 74. It reflects "an irrevocable judgment about [an offender's] value and place in society," at odds with a child's capacity for change. *Ibid.*

Graham concluded from this analysis that life-without-parole sentences, like capital punishment, may violate the Eighth Amendment when imposed on children. To be sure, *Graham's* flat ban on life without parole applied only to nonhomicide crimes, and the Court took care to distinguish those offenses from murder, based on both moral culpability and consequential harm. See *id.*, at 69. But none of what it said about children—about their distinctive (and transitory) mental traits and environmental vulnerabilities—is crime-specific. Those features are evident in the same way, and to the same degree, when (as in both cases here) a botched robbery turns into a killing. So *Graham's* reasoning implicates any life-without-parole sentence imposed on a juvenile, even as its categorical bar relates only to nonhomicide offenses.

Most fundamentally, *Graham* insists that youth matters in determining the appropriateness of a lifetime of incarceration without the possibility of parole. In the circumstances there, juvenile status precluded a life-without-parole sentence, even though an adult could receive it for a similar crime. And in other contexts as well, the characteristics of youth, and the way they weaken rationales for punishment, can render a life-without-parole sentence disproportionate. Cf. *id.*, at 71–74 (generally doubting the penological justifications for imposing life without parole on juveniles). "An offender's age," we made clear in *Graham*, "is relevant to the Eighth Amendment," and so "criminal procedure laws that fail to take defendants' youthfulness into account at all would be flawed." *Id.*, at 76. THE CHIEF JUSTICE, concurring in the judgment, made a similar point. Although rejecting a categorical bar on life-without-parole sentences for juveniles, he acknowledged *"Roper's* conclusion that juveniles are typically less culpable than adults," and accordingly wrote that "an offender's juvenile status can play a central role" in considering a sentence's proportionality. *Id.*, at 90; see *id.*, at 96 (Graham's "youth is one factor, among others, that should be considered in deciding whether his punishment was unconstitutionally excessive").[6]

But the mandatory penalty schemes at issue here prevent the sentencer from taking account of these central considerations. By removing youth from the balance-by subjecting a juvenile to the same life-without-parole sentence applicable to an adult—these laws prohibit a sentencing authority from assessing whether the law's harshest term of imprisonment proportionately punishes a juvenile offender. That contravenes *Graham's* (and also *Roper's*) foundational principle: that imposition of a State's most severe penalties on juvenile offenders cannot proceed as though they were not children.

And *Graham* makes plain these mandatory schemes' defects in another way: by likening life-without-parole sentences imposed on juveniles to the death penalty itself. Life-without-parole terms, the Court wrote, "share some characteristics with death sentences that are shared by no other sentences." 560 U. S., at 69. Imprisoning an offender until he dies alters the remainder of his life "by a forfeiture that is irrevocable." Ibid. (citing *Solem v. Helm*, 463 U. S. 277, 300-301 (1983)). And this lengthiest possible incarceration is an "especially harsh punishment for a juvenile," because he will almost inevitably serve "more years and a greater percentage of his life in prison than an adult offender." *Graham*, 560 U. S., at 70. The penalty when imposed on a teenager, as compared with an older person, is therefore "the same...in name only." *Id.*, at *Ibid.* All of that suggested a distinctive set of legal rules: In

---

6. In discussing *Graham*, the dissents essentially ignore all of this reasoning. See post, at 3-6 (opinion of ROBERTS, C. J.); post, at 4 (opinion of ALITO, J.). Indeed, THE CHIEF JUSTICE ignores the points made in his own concurring opinion. The only part of Graham that the dissents see fit to note is the distinction it drew between homicide and nonhomicide offenses. See post, at 7-8 (opinion of ROBERTS, C. J.); post, at 4 (opinion of ALITO, J.). But contrary to the dissents' charge, our decision today retains that distinction: Graham established one rule (a flat ban) for nonhomicide offenses, while we set out a different one (individualized sentencing) for homicide offenses.

part because we viewed this ultimate penalty for juveniles as akin to the death penalty, we treated it similarly to that most severe punishment. We imposed a categorical ban on the sentence's use, in a way unprecedented for a term of imprisonment. See *id.*, at 60; *id.*, at 102 (THOMAS, J., dissenting) ("For the first time in its history, the Court declares an entire class of offenders immune from a noncapital sentence using the categorical approach it previously reserved for death penalty cases alone"). And the bar we adopted mirrored a proscription first established in the death penalty context—that the punishment cannot be imposed for any nonhomicide crimes against individuals. See *Kennedy*, 554 U. S. 407; *Coker v. Georgia*, 433 U. S. 584 (1977).

That correspondence—*Graham*'s "[t]reat[ment] [of] juvenile life sentences as analogous to capital punishment," 560 U. S., at 86 (ROBERTS, C. J., concurring in judgment)—makes relevant here a second line of our precedents, demanding individualized sentencing when imposing the death penalty. In *Woodson*, 428 U. S. 280, we held that a statute mandating a death sentence for first-degree murder violated the Eighth Amendment. We thought the mandatory scheme flawed because it gave no significance to "the character and record of the individual offender or the circumstances" of the offense, and "exclud[ed] from consideration...the possibility of compassionate or mitigating factors." *Id.*, at 304. Subsequent decisions have elaborated on the requirement that capital defendants have an opportunity to advance, and the judge or jury a chance to assess, any mitigating factors, so that the death penalty is reserved only for the most culpable defendants committing the most serious offenses. See, e.g., *Sumner v. Shuman*, 483 U. S. 66, 74-76 (1987); *Eddings v. Oklahoma*, 455 U. S. 104, 110-112 (1982); *Lockett*, 438 U. S., at 597-609 (plurality opinion).

Of special pertinence here, we insisted in these rulings that a sentencer have the ability to consider the "mitigating qualities of youth." *Johnson v. Texas*, 509 U. S. 350, 367 (1993). Everything we said in *Roper* and *Graham* about that stage of life also appears in these decisions. As we observed, "youth is more than a chronological fact." *Eddings*, 455 U. S., at 115. It is a time of immaturity, irresponsibility, "impetuousness[,] and recklessness." *Johnson*, 509 U. S., at 368. It is a moment and "condition of life when a person may be most susceptible to influence and to psychological damage." *Eddings*, 455 U. S., at 115. And its "signature qualities" are all "transient." *Johnson*, 509 U. S., at 368. *Eddings* is especially on point. There, a 16-year-old shot a police officer point-blank and killed him. We invalidated his death sentence because the judge did not consider evidence of his neglectful and violent family background (including his mother's drug abuse and his father's physical abuse) and his emotional disturbance. We found that evidence "particularly relevant"—more so than it would have been in the case of an adult offender. 455 U. S., at 115. We held: "[J]ust as the chronological age of a minor is itself a relevant mitigating factor of great weight, so must the background and mental and emotional development of a youthful defendant be duly considered" in assessing his culpability. *Id.*, at 116.

In light of *Graham*'s reasoning, these decisions too show the flaws of imposing mandatory life-without-parole sentences on juvenile homicide offenders. Such mandatory penalties, by their nature, preclude a sentencer from taking account of an offender's age and the wealth of characteristics and circumstances attendant to it. Under these schemes, every juvenile will receive the same sentence as every other—the 17-year-old and the 14-year-old, the shooter and the accomplice, the child from a stable household and the child from a chaotic and abusive one. And still worse, each juvenile (including these two 14-year-olds) will receive the same sentence as the vast majority of adults committing similar homicide offenses—but really, as *Graham* noted, a greater sentence than those adults will serve.[7] In meting out the death penalty, the elision of all these differences would be strictly forbidden. And once again, *Graham* indicates that a similar rule should apply when a juvenile confronts a sentence of life (and death) in prison.

So *Graham* and *Roper* and our individualized sentencing cases alike teach that in imposing a State's harshest penalties, a sentencer misses

---

7. Although adults are subject as well to the death penalty in many jurisdictions, very few offenders actually receive that sentence. See, e.g., Dept. of Justice, Bureau of Justice Statistics, S. Rosenmerkel, M. Durose, & D. Farole, Felony Sentences in State Courts 2006—Statistical Tables, p. 28 (Table 4.4) (rev. Nov. 22, 2010). So in practice, the sentencing schemes at issue here result in juvenile homicide offenders receiving the same nominal punishment as almost all adults, even though the two classes differ significantly in moral culpability and capacity for change.

too much if he treats every child as an adult. To recap: Mandatory life without parole for a juvenile precludes consideration of his chronological age and its hallmark features—among them, immaturity, impetuosity, and failure to appreciate risks and consequences. It prevents taking into account the family and home environment that surrounds him—and from which he cannot usually extricate himself—no matter how brutal or dysfunctional. It neglects the circumstances of the homicide offense, including the extent of his participation in the conduct and the way familial and peer pressures may have affected him. Indeed, it ignores that he might have been charged and convicted of a lesser offense if not for incompetencies associated with youth—for example, his inability to deal with police officers or prosecutors (including on a plea agreement) or his incapacity to assist his own attorneys. See, e.g., *Graham*, 560 U. S., at 78 ("[T]he features that distinguish juveniles from adults also put them at a significant disadvantage in criminal proceedings"); *J. D. B. v. North Carolina*, 564 U. S. 261, 269 (2011) (slip op., at 5-6) (discussing children's responses to interrogation). And finally, this mandatory punishment disregards the possibility of rehabilitation even when the circumstances most suggest it.

Both cases before us illustrate the problem. Take Jackson's first. As noted earlier, Jackson did not fire the bullet that killed Laurie Troup; nor did the State argue that he intended her death. Jackson's conviction was instead based on an aiding-and-abetting theory; and the appellate court affirmed the verdict only because the jury could have believed that when Jackson entered the store, he warned Troup that "[w]e ain't playin'," rather than told his friends that "I thought you all was playin'." See 359 Ark., at 90–92, 194 S. W. 3d, at 759–760; *supra*, at 2. To be sure, Jackson learned on the way to the video store that his friend Shields was carrying a gun, but his age could well have affected his calculation of the risk that posed, as well as his willingness to walk away at that point. All these circumstances go to Jackson's culpability for the offense. See *Graham*, 560 U. S., at 69 ("[W]hen compared to an adult murderer, a juvenile offender who did not kill or intend to kill has a twice diminished moral culpability"). And so too does Jackson's family background and immersion in violence: Both his mother and his grandmother had previously shot other individuals. See Record in

No. 10-9647, pp. 80-82. At the least, a sentencer should look at such facts before depriving a 14-year-old of any prospect of release from prison.

That is true also in Miller's case. No one can doubt that he and Smith committed a vicious murder. But they did it when high on drugs and alcohol consumed with the adult victim. And if ever a pathological background might have contributed to a 14-year-old's commission of a crime, it is here. Miller's stepfather physically abused him; his alcoholic and drug-addicted mother neglected him; he had been in and out of foster care as a result; and he had tried to kill himself four times, the first when he should have been in kindergarten. See 928 So. 2d, at 1081 (Cobb, J., concurring in result); Miller App. 26-28; *supra*, at 4. Nonetheless, Miller's past criminal history was limited—two instances of truancy and one of "second-degree criminal mischief." No. CR-03-0915, at 6 (unpublished memorandum). That Miller deserved severe punishment for killing Cole Cannon is beyond question. But once again, a sentencer needed to examine all these circumstances before concluding that life without any possibility of parole was the appropriate penalty.

We therefore hold that the Eighth Amendment forbids a sentencing scheme that mandates life in prison without possibility of parole for juvenile offenders. Cf. *Graham*, 560 U. S., at 75 ("A State is not required to guarantee eventual freedom," but must provide "some meaningful opportunity to obtain release based on demonstrated maturity and rehabilitation"). By making youth (and all that accompanies it) irrelevant to imposition of that harshest prison sentence, such a scheme poses too great a risk of disproportionate punishment. Because that holding is sufficient to decide these cases, we do not consider Jackson's and Miller's alternative argument that the Eighth Amendment requires a categorical bar on life without parole for juveniles, or at least for those 14 and younger. But given all we have said in *Roper, Graham,* and this decision about children's diminished culpability and heightened capacity for change, we think appropriate occasions for sentencing juveniles to this harshest possible penalty will be uncommon. That is especially so because of the great difficulty we noted in *Roper* and *Graham* of distinguishing at this early age between "the juvenile offender whose crime reflects unfortunate yet transient immaturity, and the rare juvenile offender whose crime reflects irreparable corruption." *Roper*, 543 U. S., at 573; *Graham*, 560 U. S., at 68. Although we do not foreclose a sentencer's ability to make that judgment in homicide cases, we require it to take into account how children are different, and how those differences counsel against irrevocably sentencing them to a lifetime in prison....[8]

[Concurring opinions omitted.]

CHIEF JUSTICE ROBERTS, with whom **JUSTICE SCALIA**, **JUSTICE THOMAS**, and **JUSTICE ALITO** join, dissenting.

Determining the appropriate sentence for a teenager convicted of murder presents grave and challenging questions of morality and social policy. Our role, however, is to apply the law, not to answer such questions. The pertinent law here is the Eighth Amendment to the Constitution, which prohibits "cruel and unusual punishments." Today, the Court invokes that Amendment to ban a punishment that the Court does not itself characterize as unusual, and that could not plausibly be described as such. I therefore dissent.

The parties agree that nearly 2,500 prisoners are presently serving life sentences without the possibility of parole for murders they committed before the age of 18. Brief for Petitioner in No. 10-9647, p. 62, n. 80 (Jackson Brief); Brief for Respondent in No. 10-9646, p. 30 (Alabama Brief). The Court accepts that over 2,000 of those prisoners received that sentence because it was mandated by a legislature. *Ante*, at 22, n. 10. And it recognizes that the Federal Government and most States impose such mandatory sentences. *Ante*, at 19-20. Put simply,

---

8. Given our holding, and the dissents' competing position, we see a certain irony in their repeated references to 17-year-olds who have committed the "most heinous" offenses, and their comparison of those defendants to the 14-year-olds here. See *post*, at 2 (opinion of ROBERTS, C. J.) (noting the "17-year old [who] is convicted of deliberately murdering an innocent victim"); *post*, at 3 ("the most heinous murders"); *post*, at 7 ("the worst types of murder"); *post*, at 5 (opinion of ALITO, J.) (warning the reader not to be "confused by the particulars" of these two cases); *post*, at 1 (discussing the "17 1/2ZX-year-old who sets off a bomb in a crowded mall"). Our holding requires factfinders to attend to exactly such circumstances—to take into account the differences among defendants and crimes. By contrast, the sentencing schemes that the dissents find permissible altogether preclude considering these factors.

if a 17-year-old is convicted of deliberately murdering an innocent victim, it is not "unusual" for the murderer to receive a mandatory sentence of life without parole. That reality should preclude finding that mandatory life imprisonment for juvenile killers violates the Eighth Amendment.

Our precedent supports this conclusion. When determining whether a punishment is cruel and unusual, this Court typically begins with "'objective indicia of society's standards, as expressed in legislative enactments and state practice.'" *Graham v. Florida*, 560 U. S. 48, 61 (2010); see also, e.g., *Kennedy v. Louisiana*, 554 U. S. 407, 422 (2008); *Roper v. Simmons*, 543 U. S. 551, 564 (2005). We look to these "objective indicia" to ensure that we are not simply following our own subjective values or beliefs. *Gregg v. Georgia*, 428 U. S. 153, 173 (1976) (joint opinion of Stewart, Powell, and Stevens, JJ.). Such tangible evidence of societal standards enables us to determine whether there is a "consensus against" a given sentencing practice. *Graham*, supra, at 61. If there is, the punishment may be regarded as "unusual." But when, as here, most States formally require and frequently impose the punishment in question, there is no objective basis for that conclusion.

Our Eighth Amendment cases have also said that we should take guidance from "evolving standards of decency that mark the progress of a maturing society." *Ante*, at 6 (quoting *Estelle v. Gamble*, 429 U. S. 97, 102 (1976); internal quotation marks omitted). Mercy toward the guilty can be a form of decency, and a maturing society may abandon harsh punishments that it comes to view as unnecessary or unjust. But decency is not the same as leniency. A decent society protects the innocent from violence. A mature society may determine that this requires removing those guilty of the most heinous murders from its midst, both as protection for its other members and as a concrete expression of its standards of decency. As judges we have no basis for deciding that progress toward greater decency can move only in the direction of easing sanctions on the guilty.

In this case, there is little doubt about the direction of society's evolution: For most of the 20th century, American sentencing practices emphasized rehabilitation of the offender and the availability of parole. But by the 1980's, outcry against repeat offenders, broad disaffection with the rehabilitative model, and other factors led many legislatures to reduce or eliminate the possibility of parole, imposing longer sentences in order to punish criminals and prevent them from committing more crimes. See, e.g., Alschuler, The Changing Purposes of Criminal Punishment, 70 U[niversity of]. Chi[cago]. L[aw]. Rev[iew]. 1, 1-13 (2003); see generally Crime and Public Policy (J. Wilson & J. Petersilia eds. 2011). Statutes establishing life without parole sentences in particular became more common in the past quarter century. See *Baze v. Rees*, 553 U. S. 35, 78, and n. 10 (2008) (Stevens, J., concurring in judgment). And the parties agree that most States have changed their laws relatively recently to expose teenage murderers to mandatory life without parole. Jackson Brief 54–55; Alabama Brief 4–5.

The Court attempts to avoid the import of the fact that so many jurisdictions have embraced the sentencing practice at issue by comparing this case to the Court's prior Eighth Amendment cases. The Court notes that *Graham* found a punishment authorized in 39 jurisdictions unconstitutional, whereas the punishment it bans today is mandated in 10 fewer. Ante, at 21. But *Graham* went to considerable lengths to show that although theoretically allowed in many States, the sentence at issue in that case was "exceedingly rare" in practice. 560 U. S., at 67. The Court explained that only 123 prisoners in the entire Nation were serving life without parole for nonhomicide crimes committed as juveniles, with more than half in a single State. It contrasted that with statistics showing nearly 400,000 juveniles were arrested for serious nonhomicide offenses in a single year. Based on the sentence's rarity despite the many opportunities to impose it, *Graham* concluded that there was a national consensus against life without parole for juvenile nonhomicide crimes. *Id.*, at 64–67.

Here the number of mandatory life without parole sentences for juvenile murderers, relative to the number of juveniles arrested for murder, is over 5,000 times higher than the corresponding number in

Graham. There is thus nothing in this case like the evidence of national consensus in *Graham.*[1]

The Court disregards these numbers, claiming that the prevalence of the sentence in question results from the number of statutes requiring its imposition. *Ante,* at 21, n. 10. True enough. The sentence at issue is statutorily mandated life without parole. Such a sentence can only result from statutes requiring its imposition. In *Graham* the Court relied on the low number of actual sentences to explain why the high number of statutes allowing such sentences was not dispositive. Here, the Court excuses the high number of actual sentences by citing the high number of statutes imposing it. To say that a sentence may be considered unusual because so many legislatures approve it stands precedent on its head.[2]

The Court also advances another reason for discounting the laws enacted by Congress and most state legislatures. Some of the jurisdictions that impose mandatory life without parole on juvenile murderers do so as a result of two statutes: one providing that juveniles charged with serious crimes may be tried as adults, and another generally mandating that those convicted of murder be imprisoned for life. According to the Court, our cases suggest that where the sentence results from the interaction of two such statutes, the legislature can be

---

1. *Graham* stated that 123 prisoners were serving life without parole for nonhomicide offenses committed as juveniles, while in 2007 alone 380,480 juveniles were arrested for serious nonhomicide crimes. 560 U. S., at ___ (slip op., at 13-14). I use 2,000 as the number of prisoners serving mandatory life without parole sentences for murders committed as juveniles, because all seem to accept that the number is at least that high. And the same source Graham used reports that 1,170 juveniles were arrested for murder and nonnegligent homicide in 2009. Dept. of Justice, Office of Juvenile Justice and Delinquency Prevention, C. Puzzanchera & B. Adams, Juvenile Arrests 2009, p. 4 (Dec. 2011).

2. The Court's reference to discretionary sentencing practices is a distraction. See ante, at 21-22, n. 10. The premise of the Court's decision is that mandatory sentences are categorically different from discretionary ones. So under the Court's own logic, whether discretionary sentences are common or uncommon has nothing to do with whether mandatory sentences are unusual. In any event, if analysis of discretionary sentences were relevant, it would not provide objective support for today's decision. The Court states that "about 15% of all juvenile life-without-parole sentences"—meaning nearly 400 sentences— were imposed at the discretion of a judge or jury. *Ante,* at 22, n. 10. Thus the number of discretionary life without parole sentences for juvenile murderers, relative to the number of juveniles arrested for murder, is about 1,000 times higher than the corresponding number in *Graham.*

considered to have imposed the resulting sentences "inadvertent[ly]."
Ante, at 22-25. The Court relies on *Graham* and *Thompson v. Oklahoma*,
487 U. S. 815, 826, n. 24 (1988) (plurality opinion), for the proposition
that these laws are therefore not valid evidence of society's views on
the punishment at issue.

It is a fair question whether this Court should ever assume a legislature is so ignorant of its own laws that it does not understand that
two of them interact with each other, especially on an issue of such
importance as the one before us. But in *Graham* and *Thompson* it was
at least plausible as a practical matter. In *Graham*, the extreme rarity
with which the sentence in question was imposed could suggest that
legislatures did not really intend the inevitable result of the laws they
passed. See 560 U. S., at 66–67. In *Thompson*, the sentencing practice
was even rarer—only 20 defendants had received it in the last century. 487 U. S., at 832 (plurality opinion). Perhaps under those facts it
could be argued that the legislature was not fully aware that a teenager
could receive the particular sentence in question. But here the widespread and recent imposition of the sentence makes it implausible to
characterize this sentencing practice as a collateral consequence of
legislative ignorance.[3]

Nor do we display our usual respect for elected officials by asserting
that legislators have accidentally required 2,000 teenagers to spend
the rest of their lives in jail. This is particularly true given that our
well-publicized decision in *Graham* alerted legislatures to the possibility that teenagers were subject to life with parole only because of legislative inadvertence. I am aware of no effort in the wake of *Graham*
to correct any supposed legislative oversight. Indeed, in amending its
laws in response to *Graham* one legislature made especially clear that
it does intend juveniles who commit first-degree murder to receive
mandatory life without parole. See Iowa Code Ann. § 902.1 (West
Cum. Supp. 2012).

In the end, the Court does not actually conclude that mandatory life
sentences for juvenile murderers are unusual. It instead claims that

---

3. The Court claims that I "take issue with some or all of these precedents" and "seek to
relitigate" them. Ante, at 7-8, n. 4. Not so: applying this Court's cases exactly as they stand,
I do not believe they support the Court's decision in this case.

precedent "leads to" today's decision, primarily relying on *Graham* and *Roper*. *Ante*, at 7. Petitioners argue that the reasoning of those cases "compels" finding in their favor. Jackson Brief 34. The Court is apparently unwilling to go so far, asserting only that precedent points in that direction. But today's decision invalidates the laws of dozens of legislatures and Congress. This Court is not easily led to such a result. See, e.g., *United States v. Harris*, 106 U. S. 629, 635 (1883) (courts must presume an Act of Congress is constitutional "unless the lack of constitutional authority...is clearly demonstrated"). Because the Court does not rely on the Eighth Amendment's text or objective evidence of society's standards, its analysis of precedent alone must bear the "heavy burden [that] rests on those who would attack the judgment of the representatives of the people." *Gregg*, 428 U. S., at 175. If the Court is unwilling to say that precedent compels today's decision, perhaps it should reconsider that decision.

[Other disstenting opinions omitted.]

Other works in this series

THE RISE OF TRUMP
AMERICA'S AUTHORITARIAN SPRING
Matthew C. MacWilliams

THE LIMITS OF RELIGIOUS TOLERANCE
Alan Jay Levinovitz

www.ingramcontent.com/pod-product-compliance
Lightning Source LLC
Chambersburg PA
CBHW071604200326
41519CB00021BB/6858